CONSCIOUS ENTERPRISES PRESENTS:

SPIRIT

I0150814

INSIDE

(A COLLECTION OF SPIRITUALLY UPLIFTING POEMS)

WRITTEN BY:BOMANI PTAH MAAT
(FORMERLY KNOWN AS **TONY B. CONSCIOUS**)

Table of Contents

INTRODUCTION

Welcome to this LYRICAL LIBATION called SPIRIT INSIDE. It's written for those who are 2 BLESSED 2B STRESSED and operate on PURE ENERGY. It's 100% NATURAL and will undoubtably lead to THE REBIRTH of your soul leaving you TOTALLY EXPOSED and open to a whole new SPIRITUAL FAMILY.

For me, it's FREEDOM OR DEATH. I have GREAT SPIRITS who protect me and ask, WHAT IS A POEM ? While in the BELLY OF THE BEAST, looking at THE FENCE, having AFRICAN NOSTALGIA, I WRITE. I know THE CLOCK IS TICKING and like BIBLICAL PROFITS, THE FUTURE IS based on energy, which is what WE ARE.

The universe is PITCH BLACK and me, being THE BLACK MAN, I stay HAPPI 2B NAPPI and out of any type of CLIQUE'. I'm actually a PANTHER with M.E (METAPHYSICAL ENERGY), who lives a life of PURE ALCHEMY. I appreciate the MORNING TENDERNESS and am constantly reminded, I am HERE TO HEAL !!!

Oftentimes, that leaves me ALL ALONE, asking myself RU486 ?

So many people be LOVIN' HATE and DISS anything positive, but while I'm IN THIS SHELL, living in the United Snakes of Amerikkka (MY COUNTRY and MY FUNNY VALENTINE), where I be dreaming of A BLAK CHRISTMAS and where OUR SHINING BLACK PRINCE comes 4 WORD, to tell the world we are TIRED of THE STATE OF THE NATION, I feel like I'm ASPHALT.

That's when I've got to just take the TIME to elevate my spirit to HIGHER PLANES and realize that THE SKY IS THE LIMIT. Being THE BLACK FATHER that I am, I know I'm in THE MATRIX. But I look up IN THE STARS and my TRAIN OF THOUGHT is on G.O.D, NUMEROLOGY and allowing myself to JUST BE.

Knowing the difference between a DOG-N-GOD, my COMPUTER LOVE allows me to put JUST A LIL' LOVE into each and every poem, and it seems that I have THE GOLDEN TOUCH. It's the Creator's AMAZING GRACE, not THE MOTHER HERB that makes my SPOKEN VERBS so potent, NO BUTTS ABOUT IT !!!

When it comes to spirit, I'm FULL OF IT and see myself as a cosmic child living in this 3rd dimension with each poem representing my playtime in the universal SANDBOX.

So come with me on a journey, as I search DEEP WITHIN, becoming ONE with my CELLULAR MEMORIES and superseding MORTALS, and through every poem, allowing my consciousness to SHINE BRIGHT.

Is your spirit HALF EMPTY OR HALF FULL?
Do you have HAPPINESS in your life? Do you know that GOD IS IN THE GHETTO ? What is your REALITE' ?

These questions will be answered, hopefully with this latest creation by yours truly, TONY B.

NAMASTE...

LYRICAL LIBATION

In the ancient times, when our ancestors started civilization
We used to perform a ceremony known as libations
We did this before every performance, presentation and celebration
Giving respect and praise to the ancestors in every situation

But now we've lost so much, "Is that necessary?" some ask
And I say "ABSOLUTELY" before we embark upon any task
When the brothas pour out a little liquor, for their "dead homies" on
the curb
They're practicing an ancient ritual, though of this, they've never
heard

And this is why right now, I present this libation to you
For, we can't rise to our greatness, without paying the respect that's
due
Everything is based on "NOMMO" or the power of the spoken word
And this ritual comes from our TRUE cultures and an old African
proverb

You must acknowledge those who have come before and passed
away
To gain their wisdom and strength, to take you forward to the next
day
And then once you've transcended, our children will do the same
They will give thanks and praises and pour libations in your name

So first we take the plant, which symbolizes the earth
And a pitcher of water, to show what these elements are worth
I often light some incense and candles, to represent the fire
While the air is everywhere, and the breath of life continues to take
us higher

And we start by acknowledging the ONE creative force
Though called JAH, ALLAH, JEHOVAH, BUDDAH, RAH and/or GOD
of course
We may worship differently, through the religion of one's choice
But the CREATOR receives our messages and definitely hears our
voice

We then acknowledge all we're connected to
The birds, bees, flowers, nature and the trees

All the beings and planets in this universe
Plus all the energies and galaxies that we can't conceive

Next we acknowledge ISIS and OSIRUS known originally as ASAR
and AUSET
PTAH, NEFERTITI, DJUHUTI, KING TUT, NEFERTARI and IMHOTEP
All those deities, Gods and Goddesses from Egypt or KEMET
And all those Ancients from the Nile Valley, who haven't even been
discovered yet

We then acknowledge SHAKA ZULU, Queen MAKEDA and
HANNIBAL
Queen NZINGAH, Goddess MEDUSA and Timbuktu, proving we
weren't cannibals
We acknowledge the Moors, the Universities and empires such as
the SONGHAI
The ZULUs, PIGMIES, TWA and DOGONs, plus all the other tribes

We acknowledge all those Africans strong enough to say
"Before I become a slave, I'd rather die"
And all those who EVEN on the slaveship, fought, killed and survived
We acknowledge TOUISSANT, CRISPUS ATTUCKS and other
soldiers
Who died hour after hour
The so-called Indians, and all those with melanin, in America before
the Mayflower

We acknowledge NAT TURNER, DENMARK VESEY, GABRIEL
PROSSER and of course CUDJO
MARTIN DELANEY and all the rest who lead the slave revolts
We give it up for HARRIET TUBMAN and SOJOURNER TRUTH
IDA B. WELLS, FREDRICK DOUGLASS and BOOKER T.
WASHINGTON too

We thank GEORGE WASHINGTON CARVER, LOUIS LATTIMER and
ELIJAH MCCOY
GARRET A. MORGON, WILLIAM PURVIS and other inventors who
inspire our girls and boys
MARTIN LUTHER KING, MALCOLM X, ELIJAH MUHAMMAD and
NOBLE DREW ALI
.   The Black Panthers, the MOVE organization
And of course the inspirational MARCUS MOZIA GARVEY

We acknowledge LANGSTON HUGHES, PAUL ROBESON

And other artists down for the cause
For TUPAC, EAZY E, BIGGIE and BIG PUN, we should just have a
silent pause
For all the artwork and music styles we have created
Those who have danced and brought us messages visually
OSCAR MICHEAUX and all the rest we don't know
Who have touched us through the movies

Now all the people in your families, your aunts, uncles, sistahs and
brothas
And to EVERY Black Man and Woman
Blessed with the opportunity of being a father and Mother
We need the strengths of ALL we've named EVERY day and in
EVERY situation
So now we acknowledge ourselves and the children to come...
And this is a LYRICAL LIBATION...

SPIRIT INSIDE

It's the spirit inside, the spirit inside
That causes emotions I cannot hide

Whenever my people are in need
I'm there to make sure that we all succeed
Whenever they need some one to lend
I'm there in FULL FORCE as a good friend

Despite all that we've been through together
Over 400 years of stormy bad weather
We still look good and some ask why?
And I reply, "Its the spirit inside"

As the ancestors and the angels protect us
The energy of the creator continues to direct us
And even though some on this planet disrespect us
We can not let that nor them affect us

Mother Earth will do a cleanse very soon
As all the planets line up with the sun and the moon
Natural disasters will take most by surprise
And everything will be changed right before our very eyes

All this WILL happen, but what about you and I?
Will we live on? Will we survive?
Are we connected to the most high?
Or will we too, kiss our butts bye-bye?

If you look at history, you will see
That nothing can destroy you and me
We will always be around. Yes, we will survive
WHY? Because we have that spirit inside

It's our spirit that built the pyramids long ago
It's our spirit that causes it to rain, hail and snow
It's our spirit that causes the birds to sing
For, our spirit is connected to EVERYTHING
Even though there are some who haven't a clue
The spirit affects ALL that we do
And this is why we can't be denied
WE WILL PREVAIL!!!   Because of our spirit inside...

2 BLESSED 2B STRESSED

When I wake up every morning and thank the CREATOR for my breath
I have an inner glow, because I know...I'm 2 BLESSED 2B STRESSED

As I go through my day, nothing gets me down or makes me
depressed
For, I know this life is a test, and... I'm 2 BLESSED 2B STRESSED

The challenges are sometimes big, and I often want to give up I
must confess
But I just keep on pushin'' through, yes I do, Cause' I'm 2
BLESSED 2B STRESSED

Never will I get discouraged, I always give my all and nothing
less
Cause the CREATOR's infinite intelligence is guiding me, and I'm
2 BLESSED 2B STRESSED

I'll never turn to drugs, alcohol, cigarettes, Marijuana or any
other mess
Why? Cause, you're on a natural high, when you're 2 BLESSED 2B
STRESSED

Even if I were to become homeless
Like my ancestors who were brought here in chains and half-
dressed
I'd never stop believing things would get better
Why? Cause I'm 2 BLESSED 2B STRESSED

The DEVIL cannot break me nor take me
Out of my spiritual nest
For, I am grounded, connected, well rounded and protected
Plus...I'm 2 BLESSED 2B STRESSED

So If you want to make it in this life
There's just one thing I can suggest
Develop a relationship with the most high
And you too will be 2 BLESSED 2B STRESSED...

So now when I go to sleep at night
I can always get a good rest
For, all of my dreams are my realities
And I'm 2 BLESSED 2B STRESSED

Some people wonder why I'm so happy
And I say I'm thoroughly impressed
Cause my life thus far, has been charted in the stars
And I'm 2 BLESSED 2B STRESSED

My friends ask me why I'm so cocky
And I reply, "I'm not cocky, but confident? YES !"

I'm even a tab bit conceited, cause I can't be defeated
Because I'm 2 BLESSED 2B STRESSED

You need not even go to a temple or church
In worshipping garments or " your Sunday's best"
For, you are that divine creation and CREATOR
And that's why you're 2 BLESSED 2B STRESSED

And this be the level, we must all be on
There's no need to second guess
We are the GODS and GODDESSES right here on earth
So that's why we're 2 BLESSED 2B STRESSED...

PURE ENERGY

Life is full of complexities, and like complexions
It illuminates the earth from all directions
Sections of it could be better, dryer, wetter
But if you're like me, a go-getter
Give up will you never

I exist on 3 planes
The mental spiritual, physical
While traveling in the fast lane
My chakras are that midnight train
I wish to catch, but as of yet
I haven't begin to tap
That which cannot be explained

It's quite plain and simple, between my temples
The 3rd eye I possess, never gets any rest
As I undress the best, and like in chess
I keep in check, all those who I suspect
Of being capable of causing wreck

For, I am the sun
And the son of the sun
The earth
And the sun inside the dirt
At the core, so when I go to war
It's a spiritual one, and when I'm done
There will be no need for a gun

Just evaluation of the situation
And reconstruction of the nations
That get destroyed, and become null and void
When I use that serpent power within me
That I unleash during meditation

Fantasy or reality? You decide
But on the other side
Of the moon, where other beings reside
Whom look like you and I
They never die, cause their 3rd eyes
Make them wise
While we despise other guys, fall for lies
And ignore our ancestor's cries
My, my my

All of these complexities are working me
So like life, that comes in many complexions

I too, glimmer, shine and illuminate the earth
With pure energy flowing from and to all directions

100% NATURAL

If an apple a day, will keep the doctor away
Then giving up meat, should cure ALL disease
See, vegetation is our bodies salvation
Not all that sanitation they fed us on the plantation

See, when we lived in nature, we seldom became ill
We didn't consume 3 meals and never took capsules and
pills
But nowadays from birth, we eat not of the earth
We intake, what THEY make
Processed cheese, cookies and cakes

And we wonder why our bowels won't move
Eating all that unnatural food
Hour after hour, starches, sugar and flour
Sticking to our intestines like glue

See, the "Standard American Diet", S-A-D
Was not intended to keep healthy, people like U and me
The American Medical Association, that controls ALL
medications
Would never tell you that fruits, vegetables and herbs
Are MOTHER EARTH's natural cures

They won't tell you that the PIG or the HOG
Was engineered from a cat, rat and a dog
Nor that the COW that we now know

is from gene splicing the OXEN and the BUFFALO
Nor that the CHICKEN eats its own feces, like "REESES
PIECES"
And also is a man made species

Cause you are what you eat, so just quit
Eating SHIT and being full of it
Just admit, when they brought us on the slave ship
They didn't bring our food, so me and you
Are eating like fools

And COWS MILK WILL KILL YOUR BABIES!!!
COWS MILK WILL KILL YOUR BABIES!!!
I said COWS MILK WILL KILL YOUR BABIES, So just
maybe
You should just keep them on your nipple, plain and
simple
Juice, fast, cleanse and rinse
Clear all the blockage and use your common sense
If you are not fully able, to overstand everything on the
label
Then it shouldn't be in your cabinet, refrigerator
Nor on your dinner table

So get your protein, Omega 3's and 6's
Not by eating fishes, but by following the CREATOR's
wishes
Vegetation, sprouts, seaweed and no doubt
Make sure you bless EVERYTHING going into your mouth

For we should EAT to LIVE, not LIVE to EAT
Use SEA SALT not every SALT you SEE
End Diabetes, Colon Cancer, Heart Disease
By using your will power and devour
The desire for the foods of your enemies

Open your 3rd eye, let your chakras go
Live for eternity just by being connected
Get that inner glow, and YO!!!
Become 100% NATURAL

Not because it's a trend, or you heard it from a friend
But because the CREATOR said so
And so it is...Now you know!!!

THE REBIRTH

In the tail of the night, my spirit shakes me
Hypnotizing be my visions as my 3rd eye awakes me
Dressed I become in a matter of minutes
Down the stairs I ascend to a vehicle and then I'm In it...

Across the express way I unconsciously float
To connect with a cipher, our destination unknown
However, the CREATOR guides me to a special place
At which MOTHER EARTH, SISTAH NATURE and I come face
to face

I come to a lake and have a desire to connect
With the fish and the birds, whom I respect
I observe trees with golden leaves, as I stare in awe
I reflect on the beauty and solace of it all

Know not do I what I am here to find
But I release all negative thoughts and clear my mind
I walk through the woods, step over streams
And realize that nothing in this dimension is as it seems

I step, close my eyes and communicate
With the indigenous peoples of this land, as I meditate
I feel the pain, the sorrow, the tears and the blood
As i sit with crossed legs, atop of hardened mud

This whole spiritual journey is all too real
So, though I'm scared, I still prepare for the medicine
wheel
Spirit flows through me and it speaks to me
As i realize that to this place, It was spirit that drew me
I release my fears, flood with tears
And manifest all that I am and have been for years

Before this shell, before this dimension
The light of my cells, have defined my mission

I Rejuvenate, I am anew and I let go
Of things pinning me down and anchoring my soul
And then, all at once, I instantly see
Why this journey was taken, It was for the rebirth of me...

TOTALLY EXPOSED

Totally exposed be my spirit
Totally exposed is my heart
Totally confused is my brain
Though so many claim me to be smart

Vibes are like breezes on a hot summer day
I can detect the warmth and respond right away
this is why exposure is the least of my concern
My 3rd eye is like sun block, preventing a major
burn

However, confusion comes when I become involved
With brothas and sistahs whose problems I believe
I can solve
Do I follow my intuition, or follow my soul?
When the vibe is off, do I persist and maintain, even
though?

Knowing the creator is so divine
I always choose what should be chose
For no matter the odds stacked, I stay calm and
relaxed
Even when **totally exposed...**

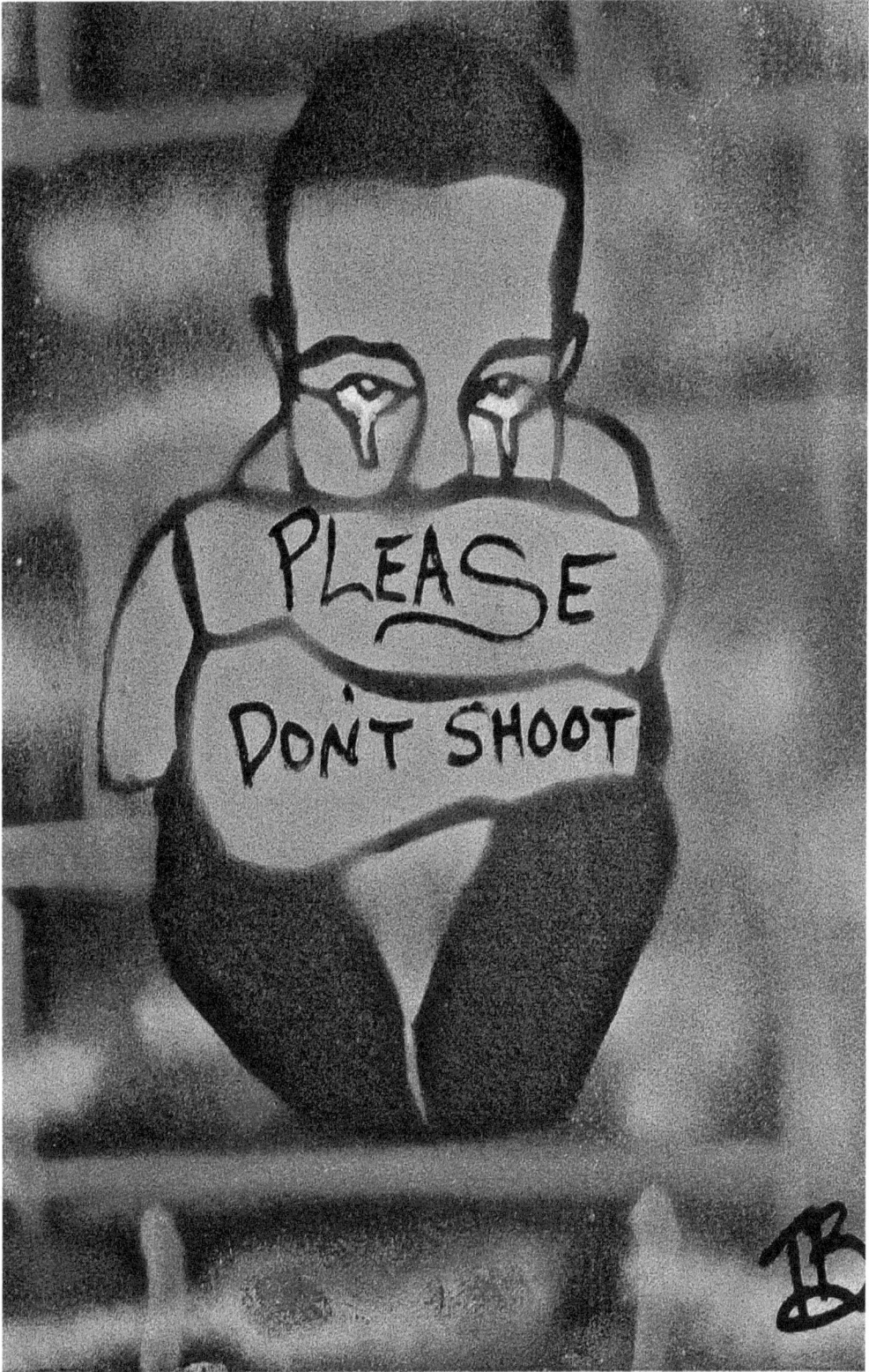

SPIRITUAL FAMILY

Cosmically we've always been
But it's a relief to finally reunite
Our shells have dwelled in different regions
But tonight they hold each other tight

Arm in arm, hand in hand
Together we stand
Bringing all energies to a head
To save the planet and free the land

As we share, we grow, for, all things our cells know
But the need to be reminded is evident, so
We let everyone know of their roots
And as our power returns, we know the truth

Healing our wounds
And telepathically communicating
We channel our energy
And repair all damages through us meditating

Yoga, breathing, ceremonies
And all other tasks
We perform as our spirits did
Lives ago in the past

The elements we command
Nature is our tool
As we now as a unit
Make all the rules

My family, my spiritual family
It's time to carry on
All the work that we were put here to do
Now that we're BLAK where we belong...

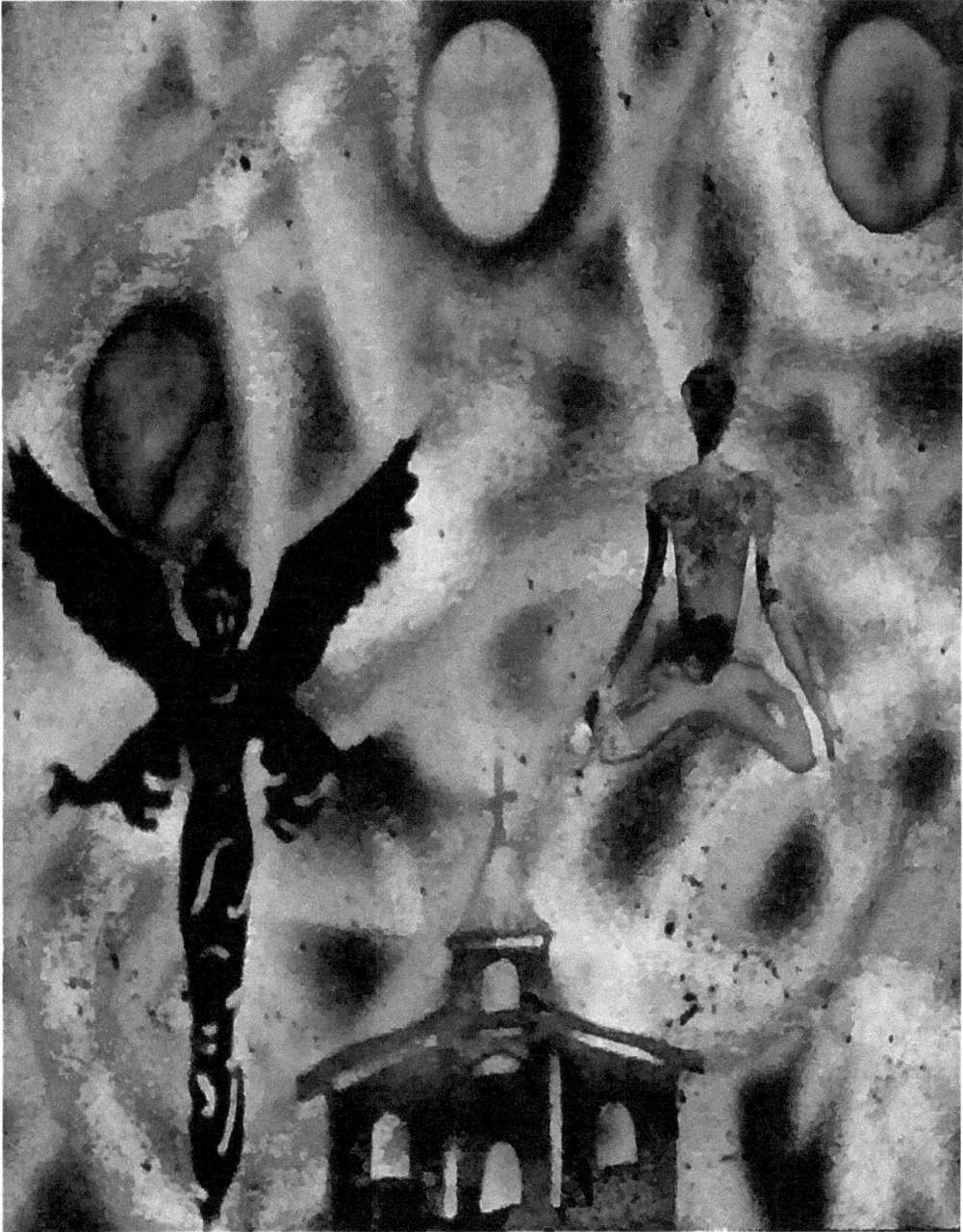

FREEDOM OR DEATH

3 Lives ago, I was a slave
One of the rebels in Rio de Janeiro, who
wouldn't behave
I plotted, I thought, and while on the auction
block
Picked my shackles and locks
And killed 2 Portuguese with an ax, chop,
chop, chop

I lost my life for that, but I knew I'd be back
This is why I didn't flinch when my neck was
snapped
When I faced the guillotine and my head
landed in a sack
My spirit found a vessel quickly, to continue
it's attack

A "slave wench" I was born to in Haiti
And thrown in a bucket of ice
To instill fear, but I still said "Listen here
Grow your own damn rice !!!"

So through the weeds, with other African seeds
I would dive and masters I would knife
I killed about 25, until I was caught
Hung and burned alive

But my spirit still survived!!!

Now one life ago, I grew up in the "Deep South"
With a silver spoon in my mouth
While other slaves were ordered about
I was born as a mulatto and will attest to the fact
I never received one whip mark upon my yellow back

However pleasant this may seem
There is nothing funny
About being though of, even then, a s priceless commodity
Worth more than any amount of money

I couldn't buy my freedom
So what could one do?
Besides kill my master, his wife and his children
With blows to the face from a horseshoe

Knowing all my letters, I wrote my own pass
And so none of the slave traders could harm me
I ran to the north and fulfilled a slave's dream
I joined the Yankee's army

There my spirit was in a state of bliss
Killing crackas with my musket and grenades
Until a cannon blew me to bits
And now in the north and south my flesh lay

Now in this lifetime, I often have dreams
That no one can truly understand
My spirit is so fiery and my soul be so old
It shows in the wrinkles of my hands

I continue to rebel, curse the cracka
And violently fight
For, slaves we still are, with some behind bars
And for this reason, these words I write

We've all been here before and will once more
Come to continue until no evil is left
So why show fear, while in this life here?
As in the past, until your last breath
You must cry " FREEDOM OR DEATH!!!"

Great Spirits

I travel through the lands of great
spirits
Where indigenous ancestors are present
You can feel them, you can hear it

The Hopis and Navohoes still dwell on
reservations
While their culture and artifacts
are exploited by Caucasians
Red rocks soaked with tribal blood, some
say are unique
Tourists take pictures, mountain climb
and sight see
But they never hear the natives voices
speak

They be too worried about moccasins,
crystals
Dream catchers and hiking on the land
They could care less or feel justified at
best
When it comes to the so-called Indians

Exploited they are, even in the grave
As their memories are used for greed
Once looked at as mascots, savages and
pagans
Now the same culprits praise their deeds

As I travel through the land of great
spirits
One thing I sense deep down
Mother Earth and the vessels such as
myself
Once connected with spirit
Will make sure those responsible are not
around

WHAT IS A POEM?

What is a poem?

A story untold... a lesson unlearned
A candle unlit... a match unburned
A song unsung... a tree unclimbed
A feeling unexpressed... until it is
read line for line...

In a poem lies virtue and spirit
In the door of life, it be the key
It's the truest Artform, for it
tells all
At least it does for me...

With my poetry, I release my pain
and sorrow
Joys, hopes and fears of today and
tomorrow
I connect my pen to my essence
And let it soothe me again and again
within
I am used as a vessel and through
the telepathic
I convert images into syllables,
vowels and use semantics

I re-create the mythologies

That on this planet, were once known
For, a divine message from the
CREATOR
Is indeed, each and every poem...

IN THE BELLY OF THE BEAST

In the belly of the beast, where I sit like a piece of gum attached to the
colon
I am knowing, that as I speak, Tumors all over are growing

But it's a shame, That a many I dare not name
Are more like cells than tumors, Inside of this beast's brain

If only instead, They were to infect and misdirect the head
In no time the whole body, would be dead

But instead they play a part, In sustaining the heart
Of the beast, who feasts, On all those un-smart

Like psychotic antibiotics
So many fight my kind with narcotics...

In the belly of the beast I sit, Hoping this monster, having enjoyed its
feast
Will regurgitate me, To say the least

But deep inside my head, I know I've got to become a cancer
And eat this thing, Until the whole body lies dead

I must create with knowledge, black tumors, Growing bigger and bigger
Until the rumors of revolution being the solution
Cause a wave of fear, send the body into shock
And it becomes diseased and disabled, Through my political pollution

Alcohol, cigarettes and whatever else
Not understanding, saving the organism
Is the Ultimate form of TERRORISM
And that this beast is going to take , Everything in the body to hell with
him

This is why in the belly of the beast
As I sit having been devoured in a feast
I wait for the perfect timing
To destroy all the organs and cells, Plus poison the blood as well
But until that day, everyday, I just eat away at the stomach's lining

THE FENCE

As I grow, Evolution slows
The chakras in my shell, swell
My spirit ascends from the beginning of time
Until there is no end
Again and again and again and again

Just like the sun setting and rising
The waves crashing and diving
The earth spinning on its axis
My thoughts keep floating and my brain never relaxes

Sometimes I'm up against a fence
Trying to climb it, but I can't make any sense
Out of the fact, I'm always so tense
I see through it but am convinced

The only way to the other side is to cut a hole
And stuff my soul, in between the barbwire
Squeeze through and keep on rolling
Just like a tractor tire

As for now, though the fence is surrounding me
And I feel caged
I Feel I can't escape, I'm suffocating
And growing weary with age

But... what's that ?
I can on my free will
Close my eyes, visualize
And deal with what's real

Like my spirit that once again
Transcends, begins and there is no end
As I now am able to walk right through the fence
And pretend to have never saw it and give a big grin

AFRICAN NOSTALGIA

Nostalgia, nostalgia, AFRICAN nostalgia
Man, does my spirit miss home
As I dwell in North America,
Full of anxiety and hysteria
I conclude, I've been subdued and am now
alone

More like a mascot, sold and bought
I've been shot, abused and I've fought
To keep my sanity, yet digest the fact
Intense be the emotion
Once you understand the notion
I was taken and exploited, because I was
BLAK

So now I long for my AFRICA, but it isn't
mine anymore
For, I am a product of two colliding
worlds
Unfortunately in the collision,
Africa was given white religion
In exchange for its most prolific men,
Women, boys and girls

That's why in England's grammar
I stumble and sometimes stammer
While I always seem not to fully convey
my thoughts
My spirit has nostalgia, African
nostalgia

And wants to go home, though my body does
not

That is why at times perhaps, I have a
memory lapse
And forget where exactly I reside
For, time and time again,
As I look at the HUE of my skin
I realize my home's always been the
AFRICA deep within

I WRITE

I write for me and no one else
I share my desires with only myself
Unless important, it really doesn't matter
How much on paper, my brains gets splattered

I like rhyming when writing my pieces
I never finished college, nor wrote any thesis
I came from a place where art was natural
Where no one judged each other
As dumb or intellectual

Not one person was goofy
Dumb nor prejudice
They weren't lazy nor stupid
Cause these words did not exist

But I speak a language that I hate
Live in an environment
To which my spirit cannot relate
Wait for sunrise, sleep in a bed
With blankets around me
And a pillow beneath my head

So different, it hurts not to know
What I don't know
Like how a man was truly defined
Thousands of years ago

And how love was determined
And what the heart could and would feel
In an unpolluted environment
With winds calm and trees still

I know not what I'm trying to be
Nor where i need to go
But I'm sure that very soon
I'll definitely find out though

My destiny lies not in this land
But across the sea
Where my ancestors left their spirits

And their legacies

As I write I realize
Time and time again
I must continue to write my feelings
Until no more ink comes from my pen

THE CLOCK IS TICKING

The clock ticks, like a bomb
"House Niggahs" and "Uncle Toms"
The hands are turning, the sun is burning
But nobody knows the fate
Of a people re-awakening too late

Ancestors forewarned, of a big pernicious storm
However, minds tend to forget
We're up to our necks in this shit
No more living like you used to, those days gone
You've let trick-nology fool ya even though no more you yawn
Time is running out, for some it's just too late
Armageddon is creeping slowly, slithering like garden snake

What shall be the destiny of a people out of touch ?
Those who had sooo much, but completely gave it up ?
Is MOTHER EARTH not enough? Well you better get equipped
For the downloading into children, the needlepoint micro chip
No matter who or what you love, soon you will see
All the love in the world can't save you from what shall be
Run to the rainforest, hide in the trees
That's the only place that'll save you
from that man made disease

Population extermination
Chaos and much more
Are jogging down the sidewalk , turning
And approaching your front door
So little time , so much to do
And it must be done quick
You better act now people
The clock is going tick,tick,tick

BIBLICAL PROFITS

Praise the LORD... Help you JESUS
Sing me a couple of those hymns
Drink the blood, eat the flesh
Pray, pray, pray for your sins

Dress in your best now, don't come tacky
Press your hair, only heathens hair is nappy
Wear your crucifix and 3 piece suit, shirt and tie
And oh... make sure you put some money in the
basket
Don't hold out on the LORD when it comes by

Wow, so much money spent in tithes
While you write it off when it's time for tax
You think that money's going to JESUS ?
Stupid niggah... they splittin' it up in the back

If you learned the bible cover to cover
You too would see
People joining the service ain't got nothing on
preachers
When it comes to being all they can be

They be the ultimate house Negroes
Pork chopped and passifying people for pay
Spending your money on the lotto and the horses
With a "Jerri Curl" talking about judgment day

Taking the money right out the neighborhood
Down to Mr. Whitey's bank

While you prayin' and Payin', he's convincin' and collectin'
Cause dumb niggahs just don't think
No need to learn your history, it won't be a mystery
As long as you read the "good book"
Jesus saves, so you better behave
Get you some shiny shoes and a finger wave
Stay asleep for God's sake
Love your enemy, ain't no need to be awake

Who says there's a division between church and state ?
Who says there's a division between church and state ?
Look at your church and the state your community's in
Look at the church and the state your people are in
Look at the state of mind your church got your people in
Look at your church and then state:
"Jesus was a slave ship and the captain preached hate"
And hate and hate and... wait!!!

Are any of those places and people and prophets real?
And profits and profits and profits real?
Well look at your preacher's house on the hill
And then ask... are those profits real?
Are the preacher's profits that the bible speaks of real?

Hell, why go to school? Just study the bible

Learn about the biblical prophets and profit
Hell, even the government won't try to stop it

But as soon as you start teaching the truth
And throw the bible in the trash
You will have no cash, no cash, no cash

However, in your people you will see
The profits of the prophets as prophesized
So realize biblical profits are causing people's demise
As the self-hate is being internalized
Due to fictitious characters, holidays
And a false GOD named JESUS with blond hair and blue eyes

WAKE UP!!!

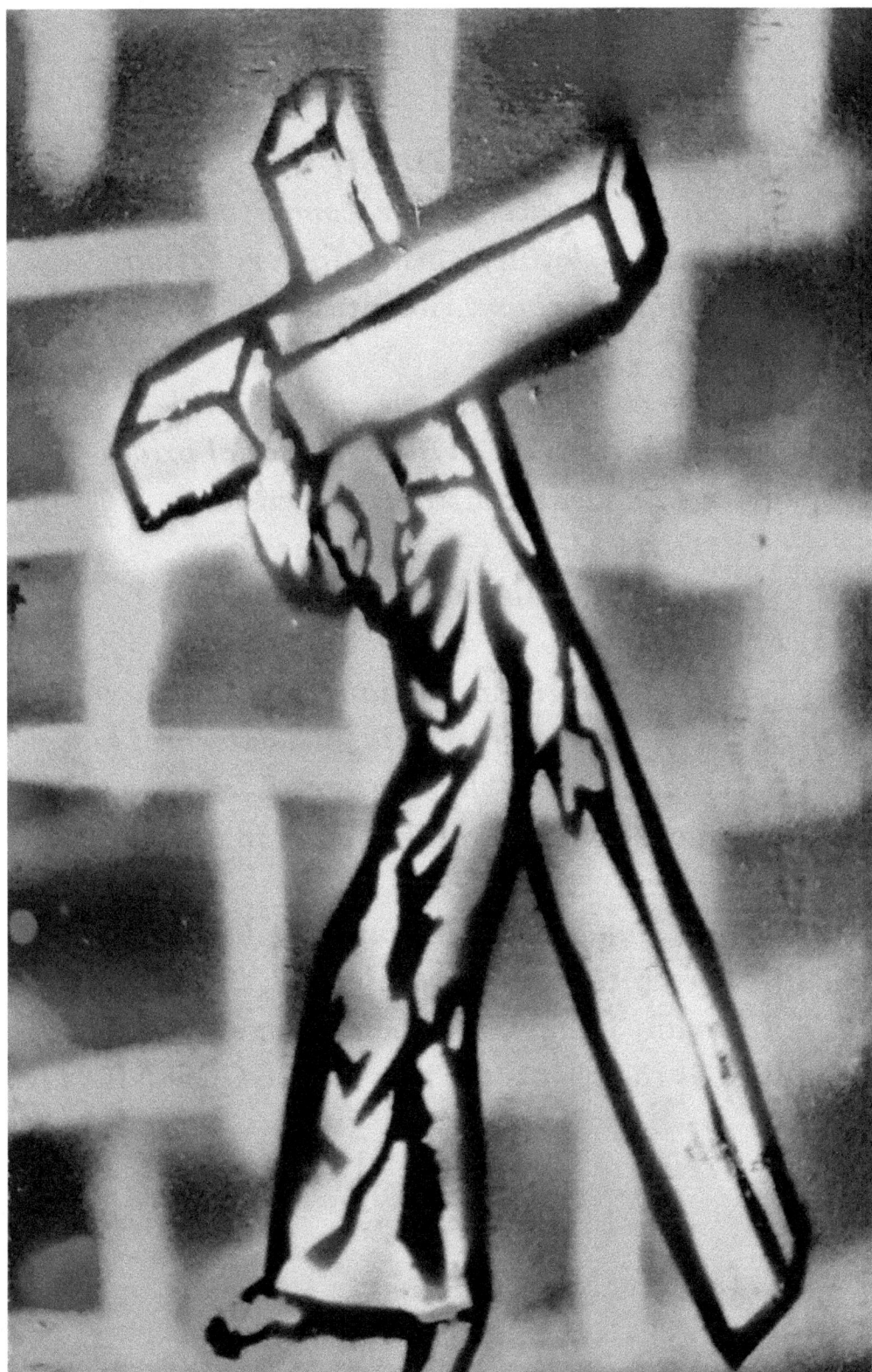

THE FUTURE IS:

Spirit, 3rd eye, N2WISHN, candles
Love, embrace, rejoice, commitment
Disgust, disloyalty, unsatisfactory actions
Fights, abuse, violent reactions

Poverty, tears, homelessness, suicide
Insecurity, prison, self-hate, lack of pride
Life, death, birth, transcension
Ultra sound, telepathic messages
Third, fourth and fifth dimensions

UFOs, reptilians, Sirians, pyramids
Dinosaurs, flying horses, midgets, deformed kids
Plants vegetables, herbs and fruits
Government police, revolutionaries in black boots

Destruction, human combustion, skin diseases, cancer
Graffiti on white walls, hieroglyphics, break-dancers
Too many images, not enough time to write
The future is the past is the present... GOOD NIGHT!!!

WE ARE

We are the black gold of the sun
We are the angels who have fallen to earth
We are the rhythm of earth mother

We are African drums, African dance, African masks
Nappy hair, big, thick, Nubian lips
Blue-black, copper, mahogany, almond, caramel
And even tapioca skin (at times)...

WE ARE MELANIN

We are Jazz, the Blues, the Slave Songs
Rock, Pop, Disco, House and Hip-Hop
We are country too !!!

We are all that ever was and ever will be
We are infinite knowledge, truth, justice
Righteousness, reciprocity, balance and harmony

We are the universe
We are time, we are space
We are the everything, before everything
Existence before existence
The matter before matter

We are laughter, we are fear
We are joy, pain, anguish, hurt
Disgust, Jealousy, rage, envy

Loyalty, betrayal, deceit, denial and revenge
We are all that truly is...

WE ARE LOVE

PITCH BLACK

In the beginning of time, you will find
Way, way back
Before there was light in the universe
First it was PITCH BLACK

In all of the black holes, the cosmos
And all other galaxies
There are molecules, atoms
And electromagnetic energies

There are gases, fluids
And carbons to be exact
Plus melanin, which my friend
Is also PITCH BLACK

Melanin be in my skin
My eyes and my hair
It be in the sky, in the dirt
And around mother earth everywhere

And when the first man and woman walked the
earth
Skin and bodies fully in tact
You can best believe, that yes indeed
They were PITCH BLACK

Smooth and silky was their skin
Shining in the sun
And they never covered up with clothing
Because they didn't need none

They only ate live foods and upon their bodies
Was not an inch of fat

Their chakras were aligned and they used their
minds
To make sure they never had a lack

In ALKEBELON (or land of the spirit people)
Blackness was the norm
We knew we were all descendants of SIRIUS B
Which is blackness in its purest form

From the Dogons and Twa, All the way to KEMET
Where the blocks for the pyramids were
perfectly stacked
They try to deny it , but they can't hide it
Everybody was PITCH BLACK

With melanin we can see perfectly at night
While they need lanterns and flashlights
They must react and constantly attack
That which they fear, this here, the PITCH
BLACK

Now our hues have dulled to a certain extent
Due to certain factors in the environment
And due to slavery when from the back
Our queens were raped, making us less than a
PITCH BLACK

We were programmed white is heavenly
Brown is down, but black is wack
So now we mentally enslave ourselves
Like crabs in a bucket, we say "fuck it" and
feel trapped

But we always must remember, dark matter is the
source

Of all things and we come from that
So be not afraid of the dark, for that's what
you are
Learn to love and appreciate PITCH BLAK

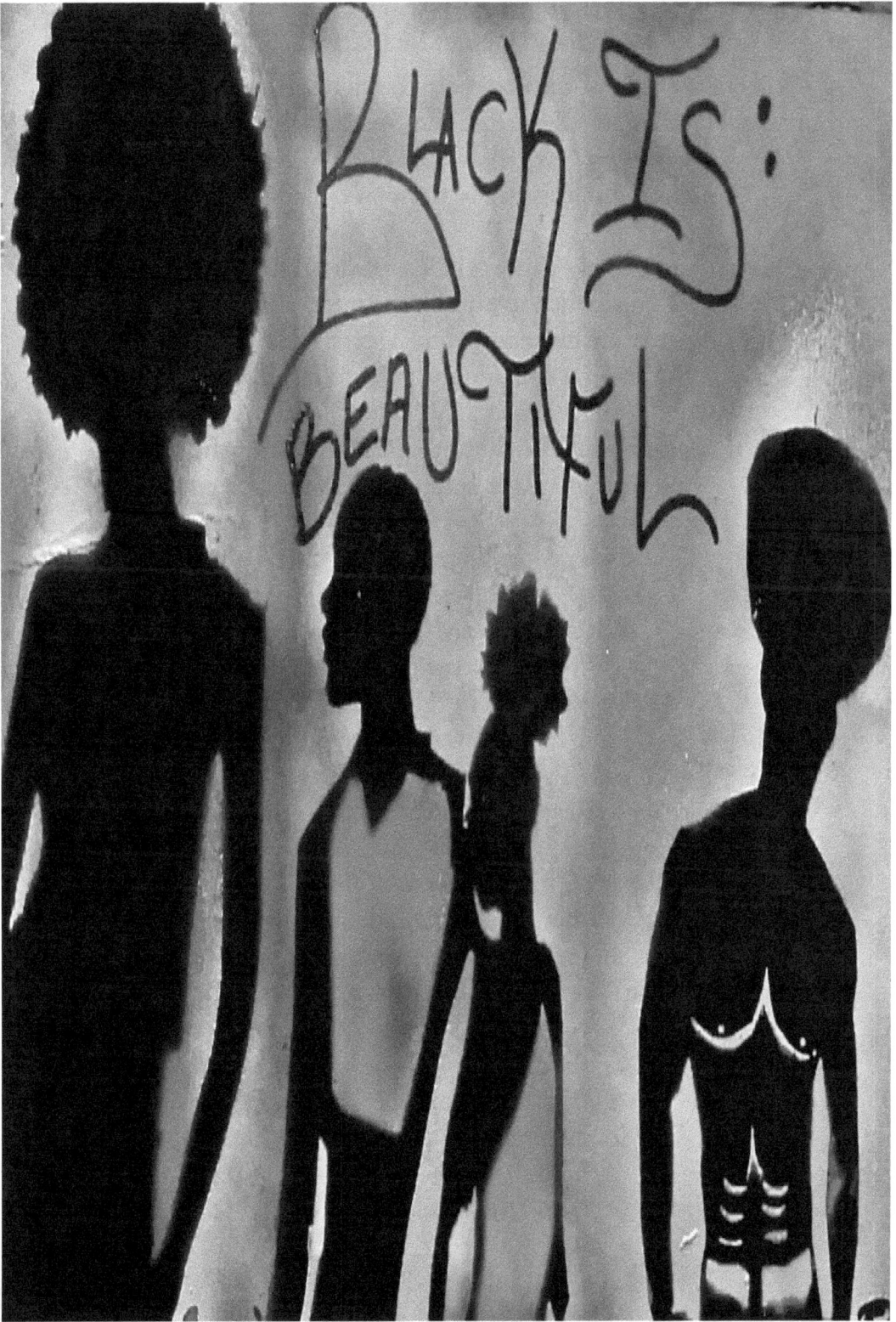

THE BLACK MAN

From the ends of the universe, Through the womb you came
Commanding the forces of nature and creating with your awesome brain
Taking raw materials and building civilizations
Unsurpassed to this day in complexity and sophistication

It was you that gave this world knowledge, Philosophy and Art
You taught the world how to feel and build
With your mind, body, spirit and heart
You gave creation the greatest inspiration
When as a GOD you lived
By aligning yourself with the CREATOR and the galaxy
And then in a flash, bringing forth the pyramids

The whole world knows of your brilliance
Oh yes it's true
That's why you MUST be oppressed
For, fear of the power in you
All the genius, all the glory, all the greatness
That can ever be conceived
Lies in you and was once manifested
And once again can and will be achieved

You will rise again
Whether it be through destiny or fate
For, there is no obstacle you can't overcome
With the BLACK WOMAN as your mate

You're a warrior, inventor, scientist
A Philosopher, prophet and a poet
A lover, composer, doctor and engineer
You've done ALL things
And this world knows it

And this be the reason
From sea to sea and land to land
Though you are feared and hated by some

You are outdone by none
For you are...

THE BLACK MAN

HAPPI 2B NAPPI

Every since I came out of my mother's womb
After being conceived by my mommy and pappy
I loved everything about myself
And have always been HAPPI 2B NAPPI

All through Jr. high and High school
All the white kids would constantly be looking at me
Because I've always been proud of my history and culture
And even then I was HAPPI 2B NAPPI

For, the CREATOR gave us these beautiful shells
And to tamper with them would be oh so tacky
So I just let be, what is supposed to be
And I stay HAPPI 2B NAPPI

Our Ancestors braided, locked, twisted and combed
So if you ever see me with a perm, please somebody slap me !!!
For, straight is not strong, and if you think it's cute, you're dead wrong
It's Beautiful 2B HAPPI 2B NAPPI

And I just love how the beauticians, Christians and fast talkers
Bring up Madame C.J. Walker and try to attack me
She did make a million dollars as they state
But off of teaching our people self-hate
And making our children unHAPPI 2B NAPPI

So I take them to the bible, Revelations 1:14
And they say "so you think you're JESUS?" and I reply "EXACTLY !"
For, it's no bull, his hair was like lamb's wool
And you can best believe he was HAPPI 2B NAPPI

We have awesome brains, so let me explain
Why the Creator gave us kinky hair and not flat, see
It's thickness is to protect, all of the head and back of the neck
With antennae so B HAPPI 2B NAPPI

For in the end my friend, our hair and skin
Reflects the first on the planet
The original and not anything crappy
So my sistahs and brothas
We should love ourselves and Earth Mother
Love our blackness and B HAPPI 2B NAPPI

CLIQUE

You know what really makes me sick ?
Black people are in too many damn cliques...

Everybody's in these tiny, individual groups and organizations
All recruiting for their causes, yet not uplifting the BLAK nation
Thinking that their way is the right way, but not accomplishing shit
Just stuck in a paradigm, a state of mind, that's only loyal to their
clique

Collectively we have so much potential, it's an essential
That we come together with one common vision and all become
instrumental
In taking our people to the next level, but I must admit
Division and narrow-mindness is what's keeping us apart
Plus too many damn cliques

But, see, me
I can't be down with that clique, for they're just into titles
I'm not rolling with that clique either, for they're stuck in the bible
I'm not with this clique right here, for they're all gay
I'm not down with that clique right there, for they smoke bud all
day

I'm not down for that clique over there, for everybody laughs at
them
And I can't stand that clique over there, for they refuse to call
themselves AFRICAN
I'm not with those in that clique, cause they think they're
HARDCORE
And I'm not with that clique, cause it's still a clique
Even though they call themselves MOORS

I'm not with that clique out there, for they love to party all night
And I'm most certainly not with that clique
They only deal with brothas and sistahs who are light
Not to mention those in that clique over there, they're all Greeks
While them in that clique, they be the strippers and the freaks

Now that clique right there, they spend all they're time destroying
the hood
And that clique over yonder, they just too damn HOLLYWOOD
Then you got this clique right here, the followers of FARRAKHAN
Not to mention that click over there, into orthodox Islam

That clique on the other side of the room, they're supposed to be
the good poets
While still that clique over there is bullshit, but they don't even
know it
Now this clique, they're kinda cool, but they're not spiritual at all
And those folks over there in that clique, they like football and
basketball

That clique thinks it's hip-hop, but it's not true to the street
While this clique right here, damn, they eat too much fuckin' meat
And the clique up there is the worst, for, they wanna be white
Not to mention the gold teeth clique over there, bling, blingin' all
damn night

All these motherfuckin' cliques, what is one to do ?
The "Willie Lynch Syndrome" been in effect, yet so many haven't a
clue
As a race, nothing is being built, yet there is no guilt
As some cliques walk on eggshells, while others live on stilts

If your clique has the wood, and their clique has the nails
And that clique has the plaster and glass, yet ya'll keep it all to
yourselves
Then how can we build houses to keep us all safe and warm?
And how can we defend the community if that clique has all the
arms ?

How can we make all the children smart, if all they see
Is a bunch of doors into different rooms, all tiny as can be
When you start a clique, or enter into one what you get
Is a group who think they've found a new way to get to freedom
But you see, not one of us have made it there yet

My problem is your problem, we both hate Uncle Sam
And until we are all free, ain't none of us, or because we are, I am
Everyone must see the BIG picture and wake up real quick

Over 50 million of us populate this country, yet we're all in cliques

We spend over 5oo billion dollars a year, but don't do so with an aim

They've got us divided, cause they know if we united, we'd put an end to this game

So, **BLAK PEOPLE WE MUST COME TOGETHER AS ONE UNIT**

Like we did on the slave ship

WE MUST LOVE ONE ANOTHER, that means all sistahs and brothas

And become one strong , thick clique

PANTHER

We're in a state of war, so it's time for hardcore
Tactics, so when I rap this make sure you don't ignore
The message I'm bringing, not dancing nor singing
Not marching or protesting and I'm guessing
We tried all dat, but it's a fact, it's wack
We didn't get no freedom, just look where we at
Racism is still eating us like cancer
So it's time to be a panther

Just like those of the seventies
Heavenly, yes indeed, but more deadly
Spiritual, on each and every level
But not afraid to stand up to the devil
Take it to him in every sense, with self defense
Make the cracka a past tense, give the planet a rinse
Hence, no more tolerance
Of police brutality, what a reality
We're taking our land back, starting to attack
All those who see black as a target for gats
Knowing revolution is the only answer
I'm a BLACK PANTHER

My father, my dad, really had it bad
He's in the belly of the beast, for his activities
But who sees the reality of the situation
We've got to uplift the whole black nation
For Huey P., Bobby Seale and all that were killed
For Assata, yes we gotta, continue to keep it real
For Mumia and Geronimo Pratt, I take my hat
Off, they weren't soft, but proud to be black
I pump my fist, like this, every hour
And continuously scream, I have a dream of BLAK POWER
Devour all enemies, i smoke no trees
Nor eat any flesh, cause I've got to be my best
Test, the waters, for the sons and daughters
Of the original panthers who got slaughtered
Coming through a different medium, I'm seein 'em non
stop
With break breats, in the street, we drop the HIP-HOP
Revolutionary lyrics, I know you hear it, don't fear
it

Cause it all comes in the original spirit
Of the ancestors, whether you be an m.c. or break
dancer
Yo...we've got to all be panthers

Now we in a peculiar time, so in this rhyme
I've got to break down to you the new paradym
Technology is the psychology of them
Who depend on machines to destroy the melanin

Contrails in the air, everywhere they spray
And can listen to our words from 5 miles away
O.K., so now what do we do?
Try another shoe, instead of becoming blue

the old way, sorry to say would be unproductive
Bullets and guns, under the sun, is self-destructive
The planets are in realignment, so our assignment
Is to take the energy and get behind it

I find it, to be quite ironic, we're super sonic
And bionic, soaking in cosmic consciousness like a
tonic
To make it simple and plain, for the average brain
Let me explain and break it down once again

We will not win on the physical plane
It's insane, when they have technology trained
To annihilate us without a second thought, believe it
or not
So now we have to use everything we've got

Our chakras, pineal gland and our minds
To accel, past this hell and leave them behind
JuJu, to help us get through, to the new, new
And rituals, to eradicate all the unspiritual

All the other dimensions, must be extensions
Of our beings, no believing in the white man's
inventions
Nature and the animals, over the cannibals
And we'll obliterate, the enemy like droppin' anvils

We've got to become the GODS, some think are odd
And be able to build or destroy with a nod

And this Brothas and Sistahs be the new answer
We've got to become METAPHYSICAL PANTHERS

M.E. *(METAPHYSICAL ENERGY)*

Through the cosmos I travel, Bringing infinite light
To this earthly shell, through the wombniverse, be my flight
I scream out as I penetrate this dimension in tact
As a GOD in mortal form, my planet calls me back

But I just can't go, I can't go, oh nooo
I'm swimming here in the water of creation below
I'm coming out too soon, it's not my time
I need 12 months for completion, but it's too late, I've arrived

Here I feel limited to mere survival
I haven't my powers, I need my powers, to be still and idle
I need to transcend time and space
I need to travel the constellations without hassle nor haste

I need to walk on Orion's belt, through Nebula you see
I need to embrace my family in Sirius B
I feel as if I just don't belong on this plane
I'm going insane, I want to leave this realm once again

But I asked to come here, so here I am
I experience emotions foreign to me in this land
Lust , desire, jealousy , hunger, pain
How do I overcome these mortal things ?

Hmmm... I've got it, I sit and silently close these strange things
called eyes
And open my... FIRST EYE my, my, my
Now I truly see, I see my family, I see the galaxy
I see everything I thought I lost initially

I feel a strange sensation, what's this warm sensation rising up
my back ?
My back's getting hotter, It's rising higher and higher until...
AT LAST !!!
I've left this earthly shell right where it was found

I'm in between dimensions, I am sound

I am light once again, I am cosmically connected
I am liquid, I am fluid, I am resurrected
I am air, I am unseen to 3rd dimensional beings
I am ME once again, M.E. , I am METAPHYSICAL ENERGY

PURE ALCHEMY

Internally, I part the Red Sea
I am the telescope and radio frequency
I am technology in each and every facet
I am my own riches, I am my greatest asset

Those without melanin need to step outside
But for me, internally that be suicide
My 1st eye, my guide, definitely tells me why
I need no pride, I just meditate and abide

By the way of the cosmos, I have came
The serpent wisdom's my chariot, infinite be my name
I am the spiritual, not stuck in the physical
I travel to and fro, cause I'm inter-dimensional

Fully expandable and fluid like water
A child of Sirius and of cosmic sons and daughters
Like Osirus, I be all that be

A bright ray of light, once this shell you can't see
Like chlorophyll, I energize the plants
Like earth, wind and fire, I am the rain dance
I advance, not by chance, but with one glance

I know no boundaries, I know no happenstance
All I know is that I be, eternity
The product, the producer, the creative energy

PURE ALCHEMY

I'm the Philosopher Stone, upon the microphone
I am flash floods, a sea of blood and dry bones
Heat radiates from my aura, my mere essence
Is like and ancestor, but better, cause my presence

Can create a prism, with what is verbally given
Words are energy and energy is what I'm livin'
I live in 12 houses of the zodiac
With Virgo as my sun and aphrodisiac

And Leo as my moon, Libra be my rising
And Saturn be my planet, I hope it's not surprising
We be the NEGUS or the king of kings
But they called us niggahs to rearrange things

We be earthly, which is sensitivity
While our stance in this day, needs to be like Aries
It's time to desire, bring the fire and get higher
And whoever claims it ain't destiny is a liar

Jupiter be stupider and for the white folks
They're ruled by that planet, but understand it's a joke
They're our opposites and I must admit
This is about as deep as I wanna get

For all I know is that we be interplanetary
the products, the producers and creative energy

PURE ALCHEMY

I am the barometer, like a thermometer
To measure the vibration and the temperature
Of Earth Mother, not cause I'm a brotha
But because of my melanin, which gives my skin color

I am pure carbon, while others are starvin
And try to use me and abuse me as a commodity to bargain
With the galactic federation, but the situation
Is that my power dictates earth's acceleration

My right brain controls spiritual measures
And my left brain is the intellect to bring about treasures
But metaphysically, my molecular structure

Causes natural disasters and the earth to rupture

I use mental telepathy and clairvoyance
To overpower any nuisance, disturbance or annoyance
I use psychometry, to read energy
Make negative flee and bring out the GOD in me

I am an alter, that will never falter
I am red and white candles, that you can't handle
I am the black candle, the dark side, the mystic

I am the eclipse and ritualistic

I am that crystal that so many hope will heal
I am tangible, manageable, yet unreal
All I know is that I be, that beyond infinity
The product, the producer, the creative energy
PURE ALCHEMY

MORNING TENDERNESS

Have you ever woke up at dawn with no socks nor shoes
Walked outside in the grass and felt the morning dew ?
Heard the birds singing and wondered how and why
They became so connected, and wished you too could fly ?

Have you ever looked at the trees and saw the squirrels
And wondered what it was like in their world
Have you ever wished you could be anything else other than yourself
Be connected with the planet in any other way than in this shell ?

Have you ever wanted to be the air and just evaporate ?
A glass of water and just evaporate ?
Have you ever wanted to be the owl that just says "who"
The groundhog, the tortoise or an eagle watching a beautiful view ?

Have you ever felt like all this was a dream ?
And it was melting away like ice cream?
Have you ever wanted to be that morning warmth of the sun ?
Or the morning chill breeze, shivering everyone ?

Well, I've been all of these things, yet none of them
I've experienced every one of these things, but only remember some of them
I am nature, You are , we are...
The MORNING TENDERNESS

The morning tenderness is that which makes everything alright
Transforming into day, what used to be night

It's what makes the whales, the sea shells
Children with beach pails, sand and snails
Doves and quails, tigers with long nails
Elephants with trunks, skunks, and hell...
Everything live well...

It is the Cosmic Energies' sail
To enhance the land upon which we dwell
Rainbows, moon beams and typhoons
Wait for morning tenderness to come not a moment too soon

Morning tenderness causes tears on my cheeks
I have streaks and streaks and streaks

Thinking about where we really came from and what we've become
And how we're so numb, to what's really going on...

Morning tenderness, Earth Mother just doing her thang
The birds singing like they've never sang
The trees upon which we used to hang, with necks rung

Morning tenderness, the gentle drizzle of raindrops
Grey skies, fire flies and the woodpecker's constant "knock, knock "
Morning tenderness, the ancestors and CREATOR pleased
Loving the seas, galaxies, the breeze and loving me
And just being able to be...

HERE 2 HEAL

For some it takes a lifetime, to truly find
Their divine mission, but listen, to how I feel
Since I came to this earth and until I go back to the dirt
I AM HERE 2 HEAL

See, our spirits have been broken, no jokin', we be smokin'
And drinkin', without thinkin', saying we're keeping it
real
But it's clear to everyone else, that we just don't love
ourselves
And that's why...   I AM HERE 2 HEAL

To heal all the wounds, help us reconnect with the moon
Talk to the CREATOR, in meditation or while we kneel
I'm a vessel and with my words, I even communicate with the
birds
Cause.... I AM HERE 2 HEAL

Every sistah and brotha, fatha and motha
Should be loving one another, but right now our own we kill
Through genocide, due to lack of self-pride
We cut each other down, with frowns, at will

Like a bucket full of crabs, man we got it bad
But it's due to society, which is why I see the deal
Paying too many bills, causes us to cheat and steal
Yet and still....I AM HERE 2 HEAL

I go out of my way, each and every day
To have positive words to say, with zest and zeal
For, I know I have the power, and in this last hour
I AM HERE 2 HEAL

And each one I reach, I diligently try to teach
How to each vegan, vegetarian, and raw meals
Cause burgers and fries, also cause one's demise
And I AM HERE 2 HEAL

Cause all the stuff in food, like hormones is straight
crude
When you could take a banana peel and make a meal
That's good for your body and heart, and that's why I be so
smart
Because I AM HERE 2 HEAL

I know connecting with Mother Earth and the planet
And not taking these things for granted, must be thoroughly
instilled
Picking up litter and ending pollution, is part of the
whole solution
And that's why I AM HERE 2 HEAL

Because seeing my people successful, healthy and vibrant
I can't deny it, it gives me the biggest thrill
Others are here on other missions, but as for me I know my
position
I'm chill, cause ... I AM HERE 2 HEAL

ALL ALONE

My eyes fill with streams of fluid
As i realize like I've never known
In this time and space
I AM ALL ALONE

No home can accommodate
All the baggage I carry, I'm weary
From walking on the sharp, piercing pieces
Of my broken expectations and fantasies
CREATOR, HELP ME PLEASE !!!

I'm too weak to commit suicide
For, I'm afraid of the other side
How many have come back after they've died ?
Those people lied

I'm not fit to live, I try to give
But due to past relationships
My spirit often slips
Into the Bermuda Triangle of nothingness
And I realize...in this shell, nobody's home
I'M ALL ALONE

If I chose to drink my demons away
I might be free for another day
As on the floor of the future I lay...All I can say
Is no matter where I roam, Time zone to time zone
I'M ALL ALONE

Depression is sad when you've got it bad
Growing up with a mom but no dad
A positive male role model I've never had
And the mere thought of my childhood makes me mad

It's easy to forget that spirit has me in the light
And I'm protected, not neglected and on my own
I will make it through if I can just stop being blue
Even though it seems like I'M ALL ALONE
I am my worst enemy or I and be the best friend to me
I can be a bum or a king on a throne
My attitude is my food, and it affects my health and my mood
S no more fears nor tears shall be shown

Even though full grown, I'M ALL ALONE

R U 4 86 ?

R-U-4-86 ? R-U-4-86 ?
R-U -4 -86 in', little ones kickin'
Cause some love stickin', suckin' dicks 'n Turning tricks ?
R-U-4-86 ?

R-U-4 population control ?
Let's not play the role, they're killing our souls
So many sistahs think sex feels good and is uplifting
But they didn't live in the 50's
When it was 7 to 10 children born per household
This be a new day though, but their rebuttals get old

Oh yea, sex feels good, but I don't want to be stuck in the hood
I love my people, but some children get ignored
Cause sistahs are having more babies than they really can afford
Breast feeding makes breasts sag, like bags
I've got to be physically fit, I'm too young, fuck that shit !!!
The bottom line is that YO
AIDS, condoms, gay rights and abortions are about population control
So you gonna let this cracka be all up in your mix ?
R-U-4-86 ?

R-U-4-86 is a birth control pill, that kills
Not before , but after, causing a major disaster....Like fallen plaster
It's like swallowing a grenade or an M-80
When it explodes on your baby
And does it do internal damage ? Well, maybe

See, whites, or un-melanated mutoids
Will do anything to avoid
Seeing more of those whom they wish were null and void
So their time on this planet can be enjoyed

We've got to have babies, reproduce...Put that wombniverse to use
Have babies, reproduce...Put that black womb to use
Have babies, reproduce...
Turn those birth control devices loose
Cause these devils are sick and up to the same old tricks
So let's multiply quick ... R-U-4-86 ?

THEY'RE TAKING ABORTED FETUSES, GETTING CELLS
AND HELL, DNA AND MELANIN THEY CAN SELL
As their infant mortality, reality
Let's you know, they're about to be
Extinct, so think, don't it stink

To be in the sun, looking at someone
Who's sweating and turning pink?

We are in a state of war, so Kings and Queens before
You use that clit, and flick that dick
R-U-4-86? R-U-4-86?

If the answers yes, then I guess
This new birth control will make you impressed
But if the answer is no, then slow your role
Protect your hole, and let your stomach grow and grow

Cause if it wasn't for BLAK LUV, sex and pregnancy
None of us would exist
So R-U-4-86? ARE YOU FOR R-U-4-86?

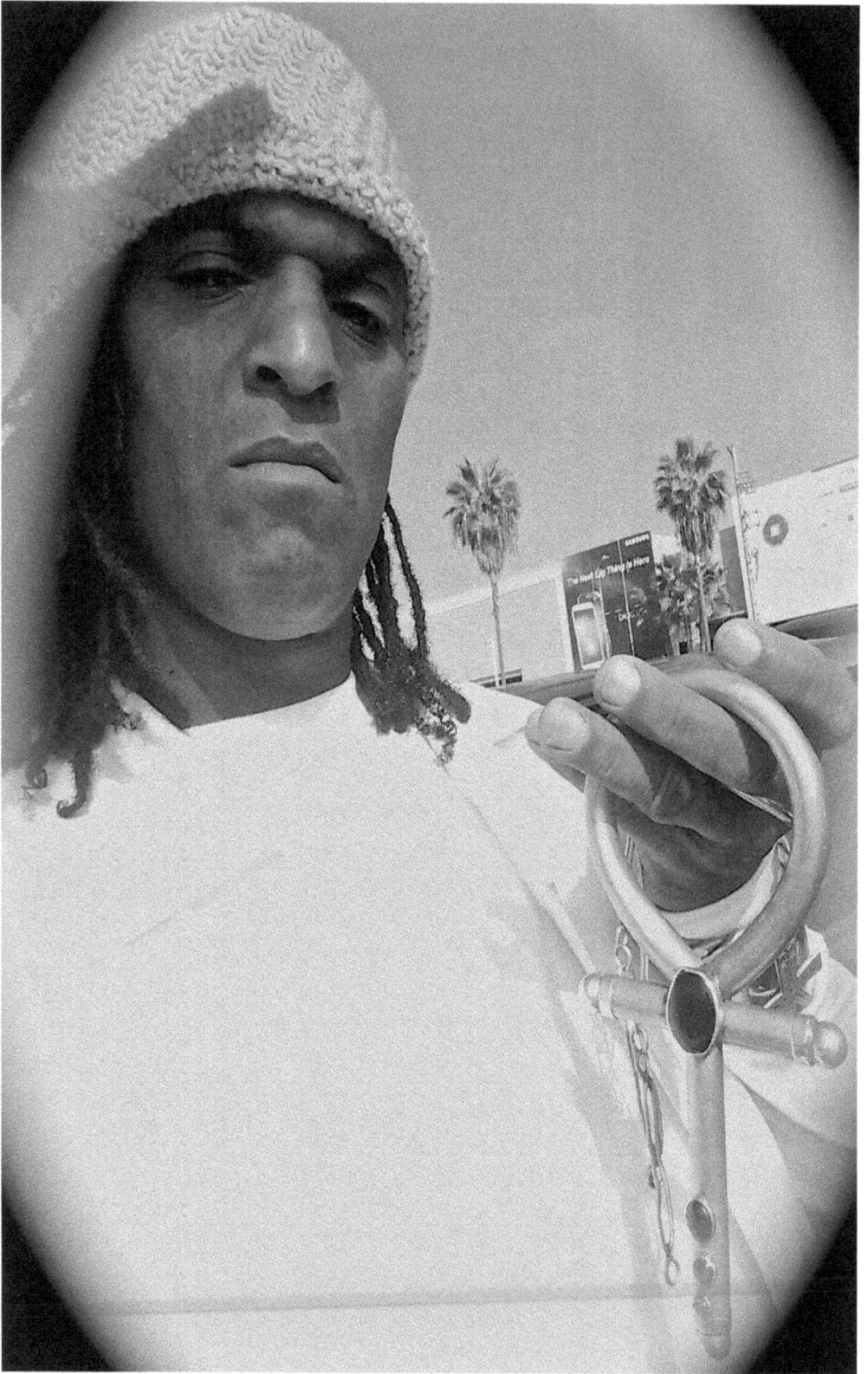

LOVIN' HATE

Black people listen up, for the record please let me state
We don't want to admit it, but we're committed to lovin' hate
Not love and hate but lovin' hate, lovin' to hate ourselves
It's quite a disaster, how we much faster will support someone
else

We don't know about MUMIA, and when we see a, incarceration
It doesn't make us nervous, we think he deserves it
For the good of the population

Negroes will "bling, bling" and talk about material things
Brand new cars, clubs and bars, plus gold and diamond rings
And never think about how the youth
Look up to this reality with faith
Cause we're not really ballin' nor shot callin'
We're just busy lovin' hate

We love to call someone a player hater
If they point out, without a doubt, that we're fake
We have the ability, to show responsibility
With all of the money we make

But we think we know it all, so we build a wall
Between us and the old known as our elders
Instead of gaining wisdom, and building with them
they be in old folks homes and homeless shelters

Cause we be lovin' hate, lovin' to hate those who wanna teach
Claiming they're trying to preach, if they grab us by the leash
Why is it we can't reach? yet Asians and Caucasians leach
Off our people, but they ain't evil
They're just making ends meet
But if we're sellin', we're hustlin' and more often than not
"The white ice is colder", and we look over,
The items that our vendors have got

CAUSE WE BE LOVIN' HATE, LOVIN TO HATE
Black hair that ain't straight
Cause that's the beauty to which we can relate
A financially strapped mate
Cause we don't wanna wait, for our treasures to be great

No meat upon our plates
Cause during slavery that's what we ate
D.J.'s diggin' deep in the crates
Cause to TRUE old school Hip-Hop, we came late

TRUE BLACK ISSUES, cause through life we'd rather skate
And believe in destiny and fate, not the reality we create

For our ancestors sake, we should KILL these snakes !!!
But the "Slave Mentality" makes this reality a debate
So we'd much rather debate it, then take action with unity
And accept anything given or livin' in the BLAK community

A white boy like EMINEM can win a HIP-HOP award
Because TRUE conscious lyricists like CHUCK D get ignored
He has only soared, because Whites can't afford
To excel across the board, we are the eagles that have soared

But when a major HIP-HOP magazine like the SOURCE
Is owned by Jews, just like the news, do we have a choice ?
They indoctrinate, obliterate and defecate
All over our culture, yet we still be lovin' hate

WE HATE AFRICAN traits, hair body and face
We will claim that African we ain't , and just "COLORED" due to
paint
I could just faint, of how hate, and you'll probably
After hearing this and fearing this, also be hating me

But it really doesn't matter, I'd be flattered
That through your minds and hearts I stuck a stake
For no matter what we say, it's clear today
That we be LOVIN' HATE ...

"WITHOUT SELF CONFIDENCE YOU ARE TWICE DEFEATED IN THE RACE OF LIFE BUT WITH CONFIDENCE YOU HAVE WON EVEN BEFORE YOU'VE BEGAN.."

MARCUS GARVEY

DISS

You know what really makes me pissed?
How the descendants of the disciples have been deliberately dissed
We were disrespected and disvalued, when put upon the slave ship
Which disconnected us from our districts due to the distance of the trip

So displaced and disbanded were those desperately surviving
In disarray, to their disbelief, distinctly we kept striving
And they disturbed and discounted the cultures of those they discovered
In disbelief, even the so-called Indian chiefs were disobedient sistahs and
brothas

So they disseminated diseases to disintegrate the population
With discomfort, the discharge destroyed whole nations
They should be disarmed, for I'm disgusted at the disharmony of those
Who we should distrust, cause they just destruct, destroy and dispose

We are now definitely disabled, cause our history has been distorted
Discredited, discounted, undiscussed, demolished and unrecorded
What a disaster, this American nightmare is, dismembering and disuniting
Yet there's no dispute, as disturbing as it is, with discipline we must keep
fighting

Disbanded were our families, and this was a disservice to our people
But with dissent and displeasure we must dispatch a message against evil
Until they've disappeared, the disgruntled should disengage and destroy
All the descendants of the colonizers, who discarded our little girls and
boys

Now discreetly, they distribute the dividends
From the dismemberment and the labor we provided
But they choose deliberate dishonesty about slavery
Cause collectively that's what they've decided

It's a disgrace and that's my disposition, we should be disloyal to this
distal nation
Full of disorder, dyslexia and the distraught and that's why I display this
dissertation

We go to discos and drink-distilled alcohol
While disproportionately dissed and kicked to the curb
When we wish, upon our dish we'd get the disbursement we deserve

We gets no piece of the "American Pie",
With this disparity, we should decide with discretion
When they disrobe, during and definitely after the elections
The united snakes should be disassembled
For they discriminate and discredit all we are
There is no justice, there's just us, so most judges should be disbarred

For, they've tried to dispel us, dissolve our families
And dissuade the power of the black fist
So we must stand dissatisfied in this land
Where we are disfavored with disdain and straight dissed !!!

IN THIS SHELL

In this shell where my spirit dwells
I experience both heaven and hell
I've learned to be as tough as nails
No matter what my condition, whether sick or
well

I know intergalactic my being be
And connected with the universe spiritually
This soul, the light that lies deep within
Is present from the beginning to the end

I cannot be righteous without some form of sin
For, they both go together like the Yang and
Yin
I am experiencing this dimension, cause I chose
To take this form and walk this road

Whether hot or cold, I stand and am proud
Expressing that creative force
Sometimes silently or out loud
Sometimes I travel at light speed
While other times, I'm slow as a snail
But at all times, I am moving
And am content, while in this shell...

"ALL OF THE ABUNDANCE IN THE UNIVERSE IS MINE...

AND I'M OPEN AND READY TO RECEIVE IT ON ALL Levels..."

89

MY COUNTRY

(SHORT VERSION)

My country tis' of thee
Land of mental and physical slavery
Where my people tilled the land with bravery
Yet justice and equality was never gave to me

I've stood on this soil with loyalty
When on the "Mother Continent"
I was considered royalty
Here I'm still disrespected, and that bothers me
As my people are seemingly stuck in poverty

From low income housing to police brutality
A constant struggle for dignity be our reality
Yet we pay the same taxes as everyone else, you see
But are denied our "piece of the pie" systematically

I sometimes talk to the CREATOR on bended knees
Praying someday we will truly be free
And I'm forced to ask myself honestly
DO I LOVE MY COUNTRY MORE THAN IT LOVES
ME?

MY COUNTRY

My country tis of thee
Land of mental and physical slavery
For 500 years with bravery
I have toiled and only took what they gave to me

From day one what they would say to me
Is that when I was taken from africa, they were savin' me
But that seems like bull crap to me
Cause this nightmare has been a catastrophe

In this land where my father died
Due to homicides committed out of "White Pride"
Cause men, women and children lied, while we were hung outside
Beat and hog tied, and even burned alive

Now we're mentally and psychologically scared and deprived
Causing so much self-hate we commit genocide
And all this cannot be denied
That's why in the CREATOR I confide

Yet by their laws I'm supposed to abide
But for liberation, all that nonsense I push to the side...

Cause, my country tis of thee
Land of no true democracy, it's more like hypocrisy
When there's no electoral votes in my community
Can I elect a brotha or sistah to the presidency?
Or does this country not appreciate my residency?

Cause I pay my taxes expeditiously
Yet my community stays in poverty and that bothers me
None of that money do we ever really see
Instead our reward is containment and police brutality
That's the reality

In the sixties the White so-called Jews walked with me
But integration only boosted THIER economies
So now I see them with clarity
And a black successful business is a rarity

91

When our people do support, it's out of charity
And it hurts to see this disparity

Cause there is no justice, there's just me
While political imprisonment happens all too frequently
Making me ask myself honestly
Am I truly proud of, or in doubt of...

My country tis' of thee
Sweet land of liberty
Where I am still not free
Where I am still not free
Where I am still not...FREE

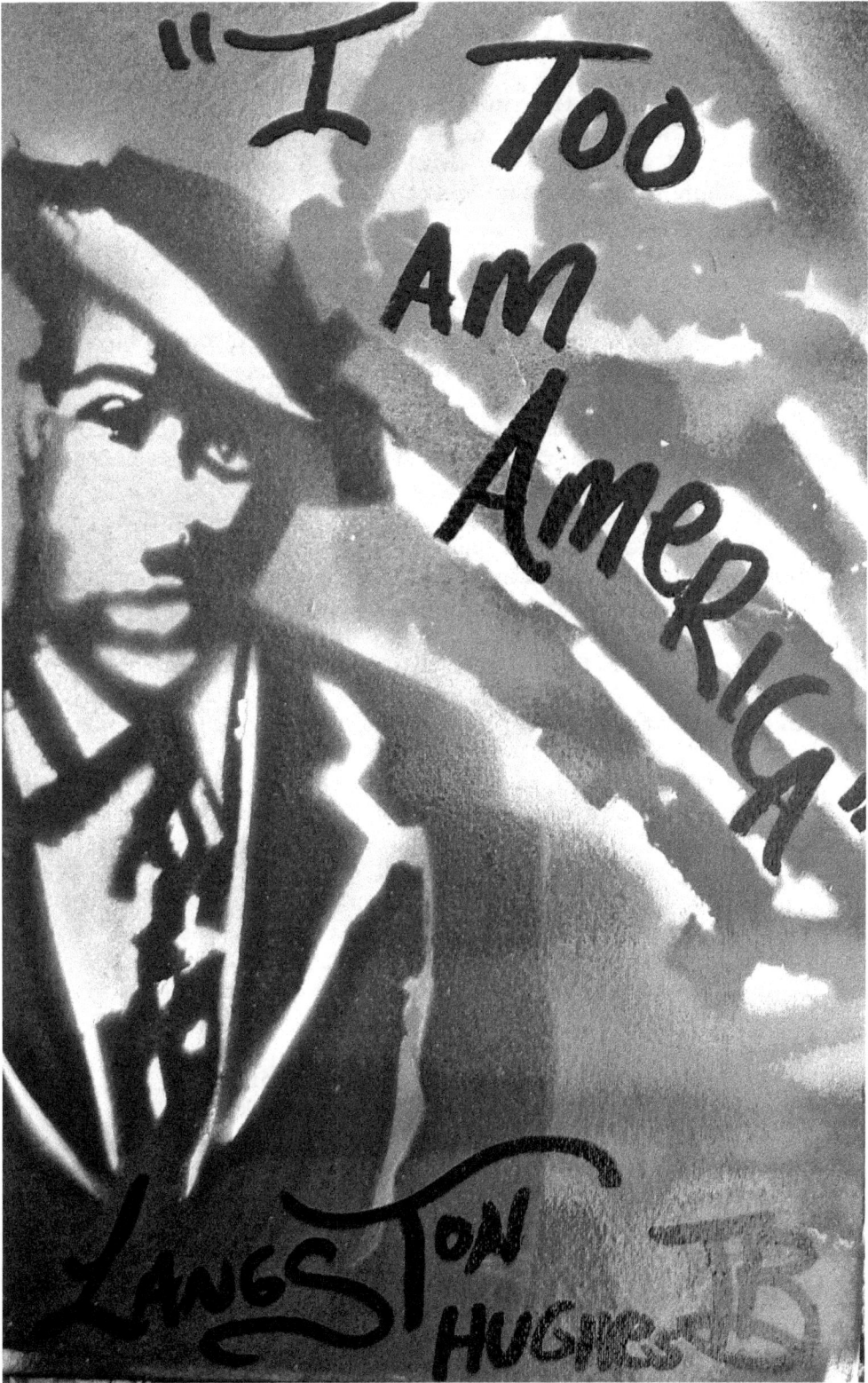

"I Too Am America"

Langston Hughes

MY FUNNY VALENTINE

My funny Valentine
Was never a true friend of mine
I know how to deal with his kind
When he broke my heart with his lines...

Once upon a time, I met this cat named "Valentine"
He was speaking on metaphysics, in the city of ATLANTIS to
be specific
Before our encounter, my relationship had been terrific
People talk about "BLAK LUV", but I used to live it

So me and my twin flame, putting "White Supremacy" to shame
Were sitting in the front row, while he was teaching, or
should I say preachin
Things we didn't know, at least I thought so
So yo, he was speakin' on the matrix, condoms made of latex
Giving spiritual readings and on how Black women ain't
supposed to be bleeding
Our souls he was feeding, giving us what we were needing
Until I found out the real meaning...

He spoke on sistahs being too "Yang" and needing to be more
"Yin"
And on how brothas were emasculated and feminine men
How God and the Devil are both deep within
And on how we'll soon get back to that cosmic level once
again

I was feeling him, so was my goddess
But it was the oddest feeling I had deep inside
Seeing her in a trance, having been righteously romanced by

My funny Valentine
Who was never a true friend of mine
I know how to deal with his kind
When he broke my heart with his lines...
Now to me, it's a fact
He was nothing more than a spiritual Mack
Using this mode of attack, to get Queens on their backs
See, we was up in his seminar, while he talked about the
stars
He said he would do consultations in private
But, hell I didn't buy it

We went, I sat and waited while my soul mate
Had her meeting to get her aura, karma and destiny straight

She said it was great... but wait
The look in her eyes surprised me sooo much
It was like her very essence had been touche

I don't know what happened when they were alone
But the next thing I know they were on the telephone
Talking until 3 or 4 in the morn
Damn, I wish I had been warned

This so- called "Galactic Guru", most men could see through
But our sistahs were naive and assumed
He truly loved them, and were thinking of them
Due to his book "The Wounded Womb"
While he put down "Sacred Woman" and Queen Afua
Saying she stole it from him, but he's really gonna give it
to ya

So, next thing I know, she's talking about him being able
to channel
While he's playing her and all our sistahs like the piano
Damn, I was feeling like "Rambo", somebody pass the ammo

Cause now she's way in outer space
Talking about she needs her own place
While dissin' me for this brotha in my face
She no longer could even look me in the eye
So I guess she was in a trance and had been romanced by:

My funny Valentine...Was never A true friend of mine
I know how to deal with his kind...When he broke my heart
with his lines...

Now this, I was told by other brothas with assurance
Was an everyday ordinary occurrence
Through the use of the cosmic currents
He had women in every city he would screw with endurance

He was talking about MELANIN, but he wasn't showin'
Any African features, I swear he looked Samoan
Hair straight not coarse and nowhere near nappy
So how could these conscious sistahs in any way happy?

But then a brotha stepped to me and said "Hey man"
"You've got to inner-stand, that he's just a man"
"Who has needs, so he succeeds, out of lust and greed"
"By talking about the deities"
"He be talking about KEMET, just so he can get in it"
"He's like MASTER P, he has no limit"

"He says he's trying to help the community"
"But he's promoting disunity"
"He saw you and your queen on a mission, as N2WISHN"
"And just started fishin"

"It was your mate that took the bait"
"So now YOU playa hate"
"He's a polygamist, and some sistahs wanna get with this"
"It just shows that him being a teacher is a front"
"He probably goes through 20 women a month. So don't sweat it son..."

I said alright, alright, alright
Though many tears I've cried at night
Let me end this fight
His title is a reverend
And he's supposed to be spiritual like the number seven
Telling folks between the legs of a Black woman is heaven

But this is a brotha of the worst kind, claiming to be divine
Talking about the planets being aligned and the energy of the spine
He speaks on the zodiac signs, to sistahs that are blind
While all the time, he be interested in their behinds

Flying city to city on the airlines, where he has women waiting in line
As he tells them that swine, messes up the alkaline
Of the body so eat grapes from the vine

He's down for the bump and grind
Which is a cosmic crime
Me and my queen were intertwined
And he split us like wood from the tree called a pine

So brothas if he comes to your town
Be careful of his shine
Just remember this rhyme
So he doesn't steal your queen the way he did mine
Watch out for Reverend Valentine...

A BLAK CHRISTMAS

I'm dreaming of a Blak Christmas when we truly take to heart
How we began to celebrate this holiday from the start
How they gave us time off on the plantation when we were slaves
And made sure we became quote, unquote "saved" especially on this
day

See, we weren't singing no "Silent Night"
Cause instead of silent nights, we had violent fights
With slave masters who got drunk off rum, and would run
To rape our mothers and sistahs cause they had the right

So I dream of our people giving to each other every day in every
way
Not just on this holiday that ain't no holy day in the first
place
For, even in the bible, it says Jesus wasn't born on this day
So what are celebrating, anyway?

Could it be we're giving reference to S-U-N in the sky?
And if it's so, then YO, ask yourself why
See, our people have been fed a big fat lie

But, I'm dreaming of a BLAK Christmas
Where we do not hang a wreath on our door, what for?
Nor do we put up mistle toe
That's not one of our traditions from long ago

Where we do not contribute to the destruction of Mother Earth's
forests
By cutting down and decorating our houses with trees
That are only utilized for 2 weeks,
Because we are connected to nature, see
And don't do things aimlessly

Where we do not donate to toys for tots
Or any other organizations that do not
Give our communities a second thought
But "when you believe in things you don't understand, you suffer"
That's why our financial situation always gets rougher
(especially after Christmas)

But, I'm dreaming of a BLAK Christmas
Where we quit giving all of these malls our hard earned cash
For stuff we really don't need, that's cheap
And eventually ends up in the trash

We could support BLAK owned stores
Buy items that are culturally worth more
Where you actually get what you pay for

So that our children will be enlightened and won't get ignored
Save most of the money and do what our ancestors did, which is
plan
On how to make every black girl into a QUEEN
And every young brotha into a KING and a strong black man
We should not always be celebrating their customs and traditions
For most of them were forced upon us and not a given,
Just like their religion

So, I'm dreaming of a BLAK Christmas
Where we don't overdose our bodies or our children's with candy
and sweets
That do nothing more for us than rot our teeth
Giving us cavities and clogging up our arteries

I dream of a Christmas where we don't intake all these foods
Like the hog and eggnog that makes us sick
And we teach our children about real heroes and sheroes
Not put them on the lap of some mythological, demonic character
called SAINT NICK

Where we teach that which we lost to make them empowered
Not showered with images that psychologically devour
Their self-esteem in this final hour

I'm dreaming of a Christmas where there are no bums on the street
With nothing to eat
Cause we know they are a part of you and me

We should be feeding them meals, not creating more bills
See, we don't need to be singing deck the halls, nor jingle bells
But we should be celebrating the divine spirit in our shells

Cause things Eurocentric are not authentic
Representations of the sophistication
That is a trademark of the BLAK nation

So I guess the kind of Christmas that I am fond of
Isn't a Christmas at all, it's more like a KWANZAA
But "when you believe in things you don't understand, then you
suffer"
And that's why life for us continues to get rougher...

So to all of my unconscious brothas and sistahs
PLEASE WAKE UP and let's have a BLAK Christmas!!!

OUR SHINING BLACK PRINCE

You cannot stop a revolutionary from revolting
And to try to do so would be insulting
You cannot stop a revolutionary from revolting
And to try to do so would be insulting

Born in 1948 in a country where he was hated
Came our BLACK POWER GENERAL, Nat Turner reincarnated
Educated and graduated, head of his class, Honor Roll
Captain of the football team, carrying our ancestors' souls
Great at the art of debate, an eagle scout with mad knowledge
He got the merits he inherited, plus a scholarship to college
From Dillard to Pepperdine, Harvard and Columbia to Yale
Academically astute, the Blak man in black boots, gave America hell

Came in contact with Farrakhan and began dropping bombs
By in 1978, helping to rebuild the Nation Of Islam
But the Ancestors don't play, so right away what happened next
He gets silenced, kicked out and almost assassinated just like MALCOLM X
But determined to be that freedom fighter
He continued to do what he was put here to do
Exposing and confronting the white so called Jew and even shutting down
Donahue

Seen by crackas everywhere as a threat, dangerous and negative
He was the first black man ever to be condemned by the House of Representatives
He stood up to Guliani, Clinton, the ADL and George Bush
While EXPOSING bootlicking, buck dancing uncle toms like Mandela
And "Messy Jesse" with operation PUSH
He inspired ICE CUBE and several other rappers, like Professor Griff, Chuck D and
Tupac
Which is why the big, bold, baldheaded Blak man's death to the world, was a shock

He was the BLACK POWER GENERAL, uncompromising and knowing the only
answer
Was REVOLUTION and killing ALL the crackas, so he lead the New Blak Panthers
The ONLY brotha not afraid to stand against the KLU KLUX KLAN
In Jasper Texas, he went head up the devil, in only a way they could understand
Gun in one hand, ANKH on the other, for his connection had grown so much
Islam and Christianity were to him stepping-stones
But his essence they never touched
Calling on the Yoruba traditions, the ancestors or Ogun-gun
He fought for reparations in this nation
And knew we'd annihilate this peckerwood soon

BLACK POWER was heard all over the world, from Harlem to South Africa and
Zaire
Confrontation was his specialty,
Even when it came to Africa's diamonds stolen by the Da Beers
From the Million Youth March to the State Of the Race and all the way to the Sudan

John Henry Clarke, Dr. Ben and Leonard Jeffries were all friends of this man
And his greatest achievement was leaving something behind
An alternative to "THANKSGIVING DAY"
Created based on African Principles, was the celebratory GYE NYAME'

He let us know in the spirit of Gabriel Prosser, Denmark Vesey and Marcus Garvey
We can never give up the spirit of insurrection, for are we free yet? Not hardly
And though he left us not too long ago, Blak people haven't been the same since
We lost our BLACK POWER GENERAL...
DR. KHALLID ABDUL MUHAMMAD, our shining Blak Prince

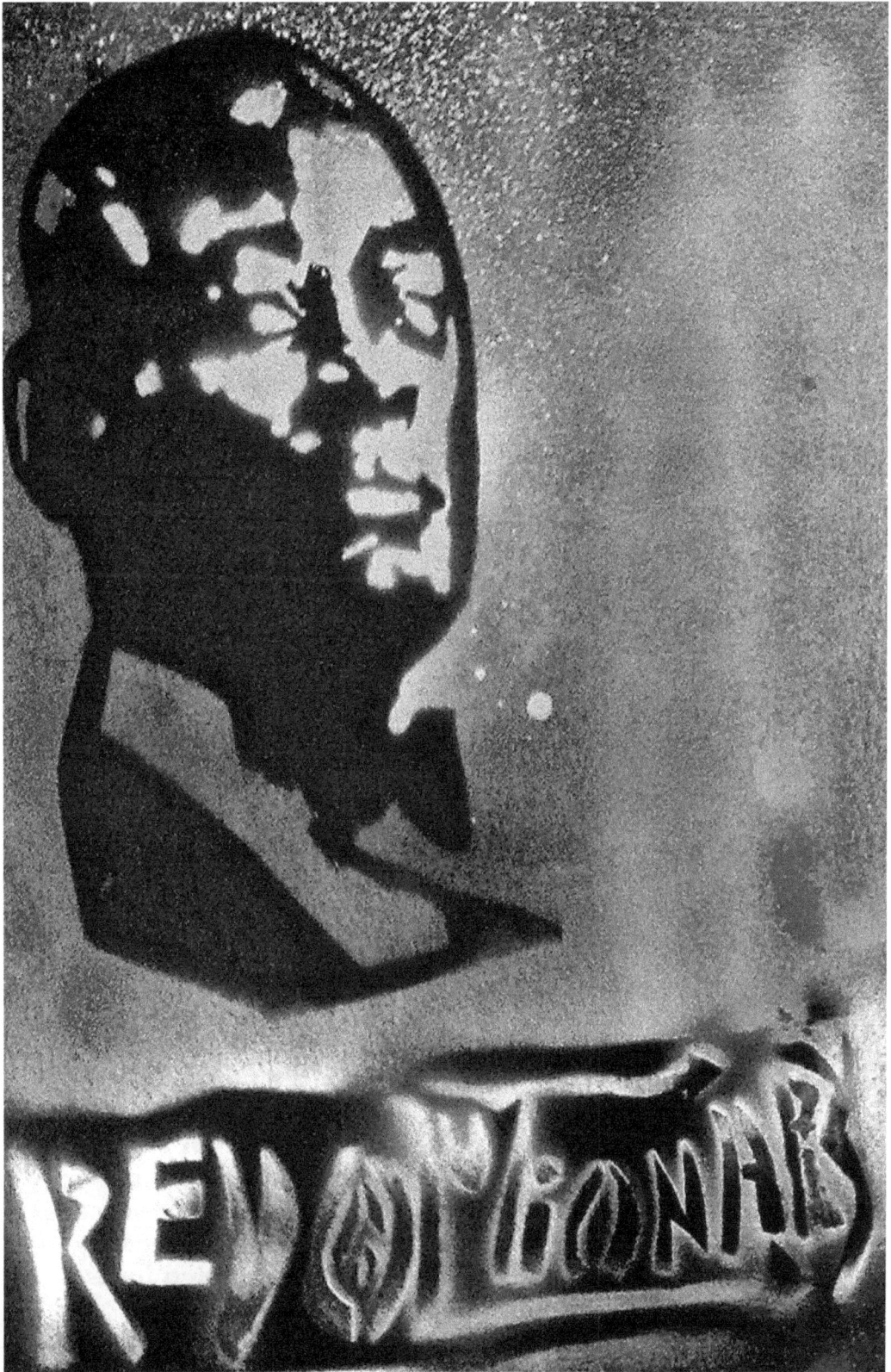

4 WORD

Forward, I always move forward
Forward, I'm constantly moving forward
4 words I'm fortunately always moving forward

From the 4th dimension in a formless form
Our forefathers knew that psychic powers were their forte'
The future was foretold four centuries before
Foreigners invaded our fortresses one day
So now I travel fourteen times the speed of light
Not in a Ford, but with a force unseen
Using my forefinger, I touch my forehead
Where my first eye's foresight seems like a dream

Most can't see the forest for the trees
So they are forever force-feeding religion
But me I forgo without forethought, four solar systems away
To experience the hidden and forbidden

Cause I move forward, 4 words I'm constantly moving forward
I'm always moving forwards 4 words

See, four score and some unforclosed years ago
With forlorn the Europe pee on forcibly forayed our fortunes
It was unfortunate, how they forged their format
And fought for the foreground to put their force in motion
So now we be forever feigning for our own forty acres and a
mule
As the fuel upon which we live
Searching for forage, or food, shelter and storage
While those fuckers we'll never forget nor forgive

They were fornicating freaks, frightened for real
By our formulas foreign to them, but authentic
Like circumcising foreskin, removing babies without forceps'
And foreseeing formalities with our form of forensics
See, our former family traditions forbade using forks
With food from the field and from the forest
And our forthright foundations can never be fortified
Even though they feverishly try to ignore us

But I'm constantly moving forward, forward 4 words
Forward I'm moving forward 4 words

I'm the foreman with a force field around me full of fortitude
Never forsaking my forefathers
Full of verbal formaldehyde, smacking fools with a forearm
From the former slaves sons and daughters
And they cannot forge my future; they will not forge my future
Not even with a fork in the road
I forbid foreigners from fleeing, even when they be disagreeing
From the firebombs I explode
I'm a flamboyant, futuristic, flat out fly type of fella
And the future I forebode
With forethought, I be the fertilizer, taking you higher
Than a flying forklift, as I formalize the failure of my foes
More beautiful than a forsythia, my fragrance be more like a
rose
Four wheel driving on your forehead and third eye blinding
Your genetic code I just froze

And that be the forecast and fortunately this fiery fugitive
Flips the fountain pen, instead of a forty five
Forewarning of one morning, my focus might falter
But for now this is how I survive...

I move forward, forward
I constantly move forward
4 words, 4 words, 4 words, 4 words
I forever move forward 4 words FOR REAL !!!

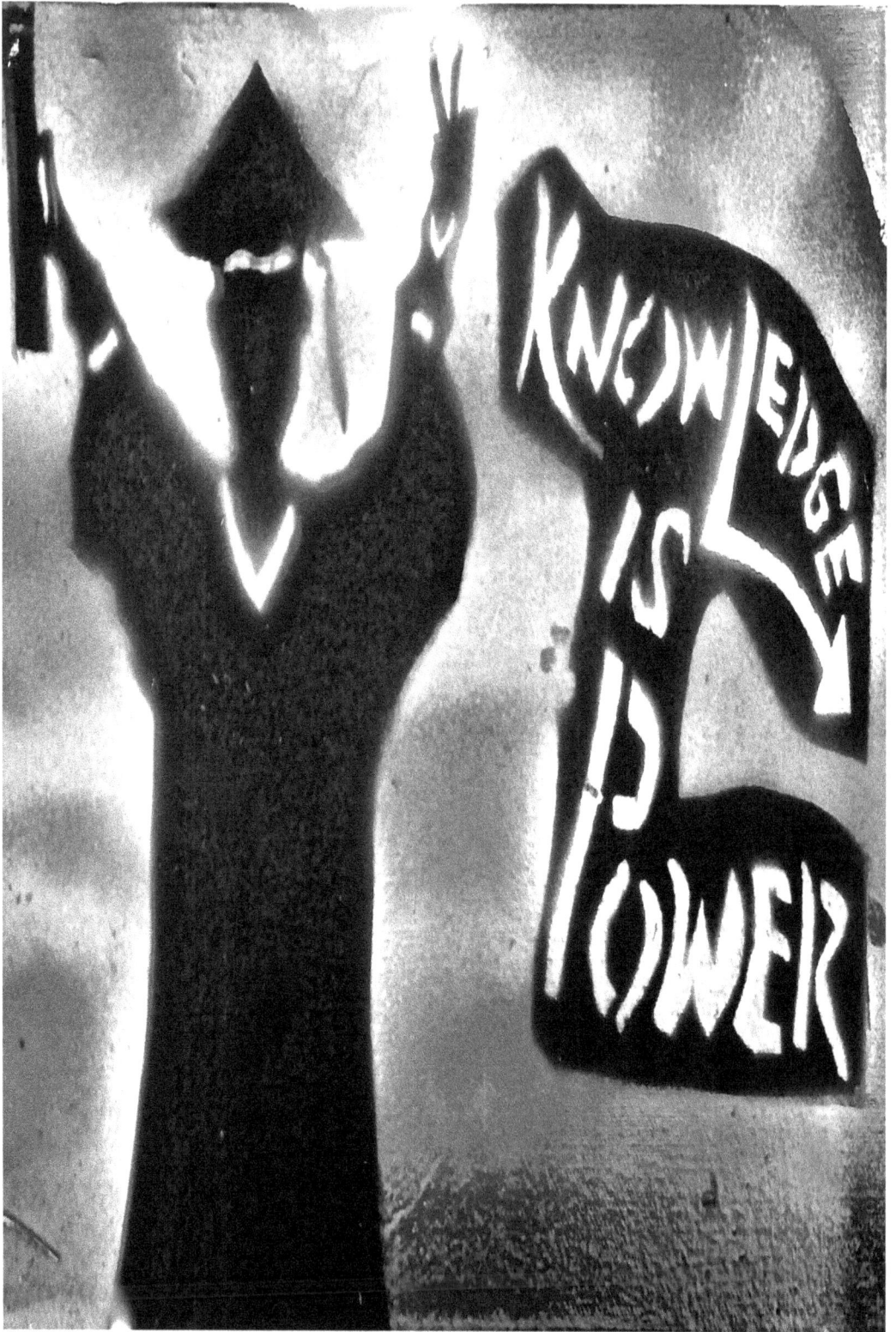

TIRED

I'm sooo tired
I'm tired of being tired of being tired
I'm tired of fighting for a people who don't want to be helped
I know it ain't our faults we have no knowledge of self
But I'm tired of my life coming down to the wire
Trying to pay my bills, getting real, real tired
Even taking jobs and getting fired
I'm tired, I'm tired, and I'm tired

I'm tired of marchin' with those who be starchin' their pants
While we be unrighteously romanced into the million monkey
march
While this cracka kicks our Asses everytime he gets the chance
I'm tired of trying to love, when love aint winnin'
If you believe in sinnin' then we be sinnin' and sinnin'
And we was on top in the beginning
But this is the ending

I'm tired of tired ass people who aint really tired
Because our ancestors walked through and on fire
To get us to the point we are, all charted by the stars
I'm tired of brand-new computer chip cars, mother fuckin' tittie
bars
Misconceptions about the moon, the sun, Jupiter and Mars
And all the prison bars

Religious prostitutes and pimps
Playas with fake, cool-walkin' limps
And JESUS...GODDAMNED JESUS
IF you don't know, they tease us and tease us
Cause the CHRIST consciousness is within
And that unmelanated mutoid sees this

I'm tired of telling people it's metaphysical
While brothas and sistahs act tickled
And keep implanting silicone, having sex over phones
Shakin' at the clubs, not truly showin' love
Giving every excuse why straight hair is alright

It's not right, it's not right, it's not right
You're not white, you're not white, so it's not right
I'm tired of tight jeans on our Queens
Wearing diamonds and pearls
Both acting and dressing like piss poor imitations of white girls
Creator, take me home, take me home
As I sit in front of my alter and chant OHM...

I have cried so many tears, overcome my fears
But I still feel alone, so please take me home
As I sit in front of my altar and say ohm...

I'm tired of brothas disrepectin', emasculated yet still flexin'
Neglectin' the warrior, injecting our sistahs and little boys
With this western man's materialism, new set of values, anti
vegetarianism
Bling, bling, diamond ring, bud is king
Numb the pain, cocaine veins, need I go on and on
As I sit in front of my altar and go Ohm...

I know I'm just exhausted, cause of the ancestors I admire
Working for free in the fields, running for freedom to the north
Going back and forth, now they were tired
I'm just ready to go to the next dimension
Something, somewhere, another extension much, much higher
I'm ready, CREATOR, I'm finally ready
Cause, I'm so, so tired

So I just sit silent and calm
In front of my altar and go ohm...

STATE OF THE NATION

In a world full of idiots, prophets are looked at as being insane
The masses sit on their Asses
And are lead to the slaughterhouse instead of using thier brains
Idiots worship a god and religion, appointed by their oppressor
While weaklings have every excuse
Why not to strike back against their aggressor

Marxism, Capitalism, Communism and Socialism
All try to convert the originals from thier spirituality
To ideological religions
What is it with them?
As Kwame Nkrumah, Patrice Lumumba and Marcus Garvey found out
A devil is a devil is Beelzebub is Satan without a doubt

Pan Africanism is the fundamental belief
That African People all over should be united
Independent and free of European colonies
Just like the opposing views of Dubois and Booker T
Integration is Disintegration when it comes to African peoples destiny

If only Martin had studied the independence Movement of Ghana
His relationship would've changed with that crack Bull Connor
We want to Once again see the light, not be stuck in the dark
We want true independence from imperialism
As stated by John Henry Clarke

Whether it means constant struggle from the cradle to the grave

Or all out anarchy, I refuse to be a slave

But the masses of our people don't even take this into consideration

They are just literally walking dead and this be the state of the nation

ASPHALT

MELTED BE MY SOUL INTO ASPHALT
MELTED BE MY SOUL INTO ASPHALT
MELTED BE MY SOUL INTO ASPHALT
BUT IT AIN'T MY FAULT, IT AIN'T MY FAULT, IT AINT MY FAULT

Concrete jungles sit upon sacred ground
As intergalactic melanated GODS have been torn down
We were once earthbound
From Lumaria to Atlantis, traveling at the speed of sound
Now how that sound? Is it really that profound?
Cause we existed eons before those peons were around...

Our Auras be like solar powered force fields, guaranteed to
heal
Our psychic abilities, when used with humility
Can estimate the return of Ezekiel's wheel
From Drakonians,Typhonians, Reptilians, all the way to the
Semites
I Ching to Buddha to Confucius, it's useless to insist they
were of the light

With chakras spinning, yes they were lit up inside with
kundalini fire
But if you do your history it will be no mystery
Bluer than Blak beings are responsible for all the great
empires
So my soul be the tint of tar, beyond the blanket behind
the stars
More melanated that midnight on mars
22 black holes away, if you can astral travel that far

And as above also is below
This be the case in all things you know
The world is just an illusion and as you grow
You'll realize it's just a mirror of what's inside your
soul

Millenniums before Maat, many moons before the Moors
We were the AntiGODs, superseding synagogues, living
tranquil, void of war
The female energy created all that's conceivable and you
know what's wild?
The whole ecological system on this planet was created
through her menstrual cycle

So I submit on a cellular level, while stuck in this
metaphysical matrix
For I'm an ancient being trapped in a 3rd dimensional dream
And I hate it, I hate it, I hate it
Because:

MELTED BE MY SOUL INTO ASPHALT
MELTED BE MY SOUL INTO ASPHALT
MELTED BE MY SOUL INTO ASPHALT
BUT IT AIN'T MY FAULT, IT AIN'T MY FAULT, IT AINT MY FAULT

Concrete jungles sit upon sacred ground
As intergalactic melanated GODS have been torn down
We were once earthbound
From Lumaria to Atlantis, traveling at the speed of sound
Now how that sound? Is it really that profound?
Cause we existed eons before those peons were around...

TIME

I am the cosmic constellations formed eons ago
Gases transformed into matter, liquid froze into snow
Unexplainable through Roman numerals, letters, periods and commas
Existing infinitely, preceding predictions pronounced by Nostradamus

Buried I be, like Atlantis, transferred through the use of the tongue
Like the reversal of the poles and ozone layer holes, I am ancient yet young
Always circular, never linear, I've left legacies yet undetected
Kemetic calendars, sacred geometry and the I Ching all have been affected

Prophesies perpetuating prehistoric pyramidic periods
I've produced powerful people
From the Dravidians to Sanskrit before Indo-European invasions
I've foretold of evil

And now on all planes of existence, immeasurable, I continue to flow
Like feminine energy and the principle of polarities, I am void of ego
The interdimensional ALL I am, perceived by the earth's rotation
I exist in different degrees, with different sets of properties
Depending on the situation

I am nature in its purest form, Pleiades, Sirius and beyond
If it can be conceived, I'm beyond one's beliefs
Because forever I've come and gone
NINE HUNDRED BILLION LIGHT YEARS and counting is just a blink in my mind
I'm the Alpha and Omega, the beginning and end, I am infinity squared

I AM TIME...

HIGHER PLANES

Eons of existence dictate the life we live
Ancient Hermetic wisdom through verse is what I give
Darwinism is false, as our eastern prophets show
We are genetically immortal, with DNA descending from
the cosmos

See we be ALL connected to the ALL the elements, ether
and nature
From black holes to quasars, molecules to mountains
And vehicles of light to vapors
The super-conscoious mind to the subconscious, one
thing we have in common
Is we have the ability to enhance our perceptions like
the Buddhist, Sufi and the Shaman

From Tehuti's prophecies and universal laws, the
axioms of all existence
Meditation, Yoga, Taoism and Hinduism Will align our
spirits with little resistance
The Western man has no idea of the world's power
He operates through invasions and defiance
But the principles of polarities and cause and effect
Have been operating way before his science

And AS ABOVE ALSO BELOW, WHAT YOU SEW, YOU SHALL REAP
The law of KARMA, EVERYTHING HAS DUALITY
And ALL THINGS ARE IN MOTION CONSTANTLY

MALE AND FEMALE ENERGY EXIST ON EVERY PLANE
WHILE THE ALL IS THE GREAT MIND
EVERYTHING IS EVERYTHING, THE COSMOS IS INFINITE
And can't be measured by time

THE BODY IS A MICROCOSM OF THE MACROCOSM
And TRUE DIVINITY HAS NO TITLE
I AM THE TEMPLE, YOU ARE THE CHURCH
WE ARE THE TORAH, THE KORAN AND THE BIBLE

From BRAHMA to KALI, KRISHNA to OGUN
AMEN RA to ASAR and ASET

The next galactic cycle will be of spiritual purification
As was foretold in the ancient texts

So studies the energy grid once hid, and migrate towards a vortex
And let the electromagnetic energy of the planet
Rise from the base of your spine to the top of your neck

And then and ONLY then will you achieve, all that you desire
Transformation and elevation to new dimensions
Plus a vibrational level much, much higher

THE SKY IS THE LIMIT

*As I recognize that I am connected to the
infinite
Deep inside, I realize*
THE SKY IS THE LIMIT

*My existence is mine to define without
limitation
My soul be the transportation, and my spirit
the motivation*

*There are no obstacles I cannot overcome
with concentration
The possibilities are endless, as I prevail in
ALL situations*

*If I believe, I can achieve my highest
aspirations
For, those who came before me have already
laid the foundations*

*So I travel not by my five senses, on my road
to heaven
The CREATOR be my guide, as I glide, using
senses six and seven*

Manifesting that heavenly state in this realm
that I dwell in
Has nothing to do with the outer being, but
what I am within

I am the beauty, the purity, the essence of all
that was and is
While strength, determination, focus and faith
govern how I live
And even though I may leave this place at any
given minute
As long as I'm here, I shall have no fears
For, **THE SKY IS THE LIMIT**

THE BLACK FATHER

To this planet you came forth
After nine months underwater

To become the seed, our **QUEENS** need
To give birth to strong sons and daughters

As the builder of civilizations
The creator of all the great tribes
You've written history and changed the world
With the **BLACK WOMAN** at your side

You teach our children self-defense
Discipline, respect and common sense
You're not only a lover, protector and provider
You're a companion, problem solver and a serious fighter

Though at times systematically
You are removed or chased from the home
Your spirit is always present
And never is the family alone

Whether it be raising your offspring by yourself
And or working a job or two
You never fail to manifest
That **GOD** deep inside of you

You are an inspiration to our nation
As a man and a martyr
You are a proud, determined and dedicated KING

You are righteous and THE BLACK

FATHER

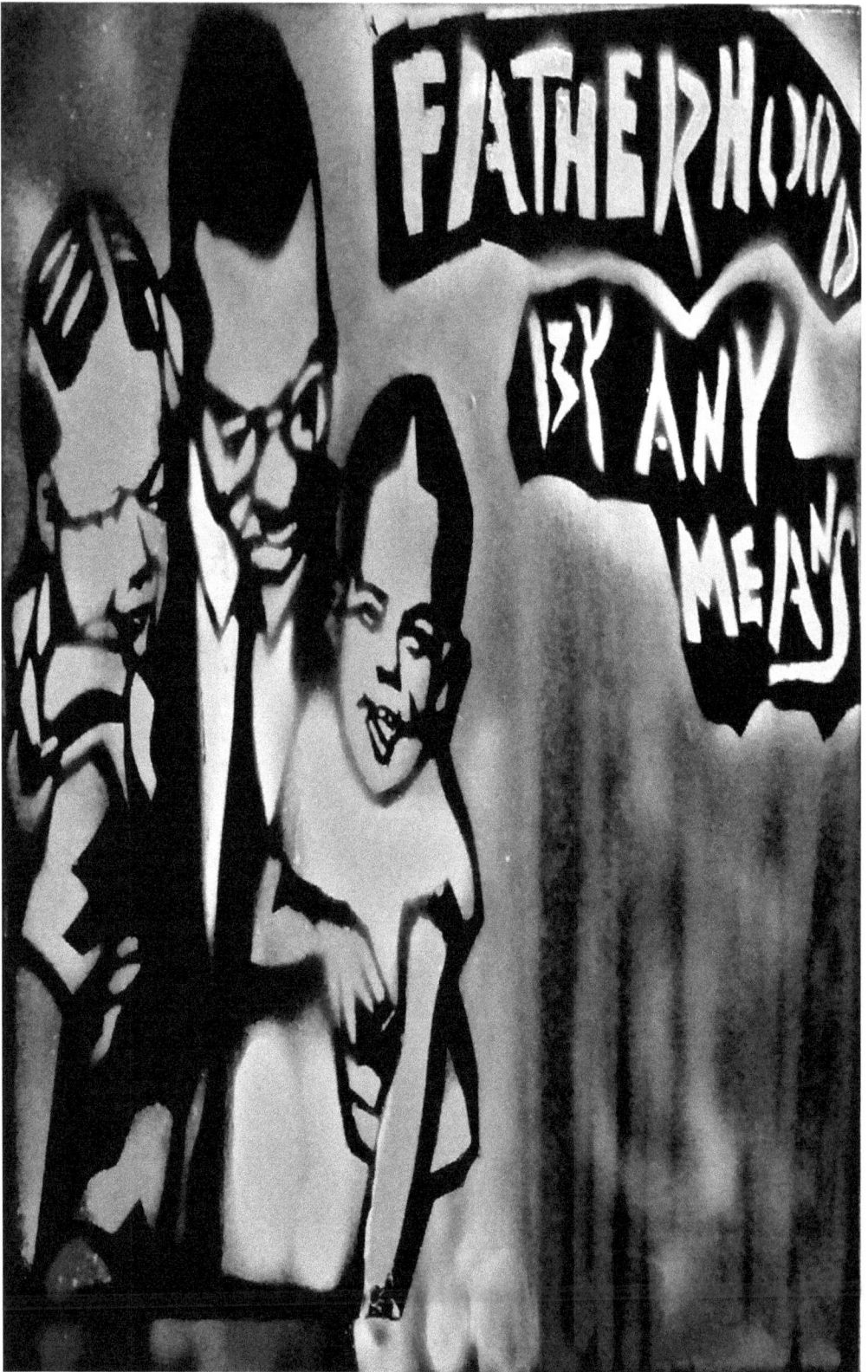

FATHERHOOD BY ANY MEANS

THE MATRIX

We're living in a world that makes you feel trapped
With a social security number, birth certificate and
income tax
Surveillance everywhere, yet some don't have a clue
Are you watching your TV? Or is that cable box
watching you
Contrails in the air, microwaves and radiation in your
home
Genetically modified foods that you just can't leave
alone
And with all the experimental diseases
And vaccinations that make you sick
You keep wondering what's going on, but this is it.

You're caught up in the MATRIX...

Now you've lost your connection, with nature and earth
mother
Living on concrete and under your feet, you've got soles
of rubber
You're always covered up and never exposed to the sun
Inhibiting your melanin, knowing within, that's not
where you come from
Man made religion is dumbing you down, and got you
afraid of the stars
As you watch movies about mars, but don't know who
or what you are
The preacher is a liar, got you waiting for a messiah
While your critical thinking is gone, so your spirituality
gets no higher

And deep inside he's got you believing, that once you die that's it
You're a victim of indoctrination and it's like this...

You're caught up in the MATRIX...

YOU'VE GOT TO BREAK FREE, AND TRULY LET GO
OF THIS 3RD DIMENSIONAL REALITY, THAT
REALLY ISN'T SO
TAKE OFF YOUR BLINDERS AND THEN YOU'LL
TRULY SEE
THE CREATOR WITHIN, IS YOUR ONLY TRUE
FRIEND
SO JUST BE

OUT OF THE MATRIX
Cuz, You're caught up in the MATRIX....
You're caught up in the MATRIX...

IN THE STARS

Spirits travel from distances both near and far
To connect and resurrect right here where we are
For some the road is rugged, leaving bruises and scars
And even breaking down those energies not up to par

Considering all these factors one cannot disregard
Existence on this plane shouldn't be that hard
Despite all of the traps and pacifiers
Like money, sex, drugs and cars
The CREATOR gives us a choice
Life or death, freedom or bars

See, our ancestors worked in fields, houses and yards
And were beaten, raped, lynched
Feathered and tarred
So that we'd have the courage
Determination and heart
Plus knowledge, wisdom, intellect
And also street smarts

This is why it's essential that we ALL do our part
As connected spirits to create positive energy
Wherever we are
For, we've been chosen to be the enlightened ones
And the best by far
Who will once again bring heaven to earth?
Cause it's written in the stars...

TRAIN OF THOUGHT

What I am and what I am not
All depends upon my train of thought
PEACE, LOVE and PROSPERITY are mine for
the taking
If in my subconscious, this I'm constantly thinking

All the abundance in the Universe can be mine
As long as that affirmation, I repeat in my mind
There is no task unachievable on this plane
With positive energy flowing through my brain

See, the Divine Intelligence guides my every
motion
And I move fluidly like the waves that caress the
ocean
If spirit is first and I give my devotion
My words and actions shall manifest LOVE
Just like a magic potion

But all this depends upon my personal perception
And my cosmic connection, which insures my
protection
For, divinity and destiny can't be taught nor bought
So it's all up to me, and my TRAIN OF
THOUGHT....

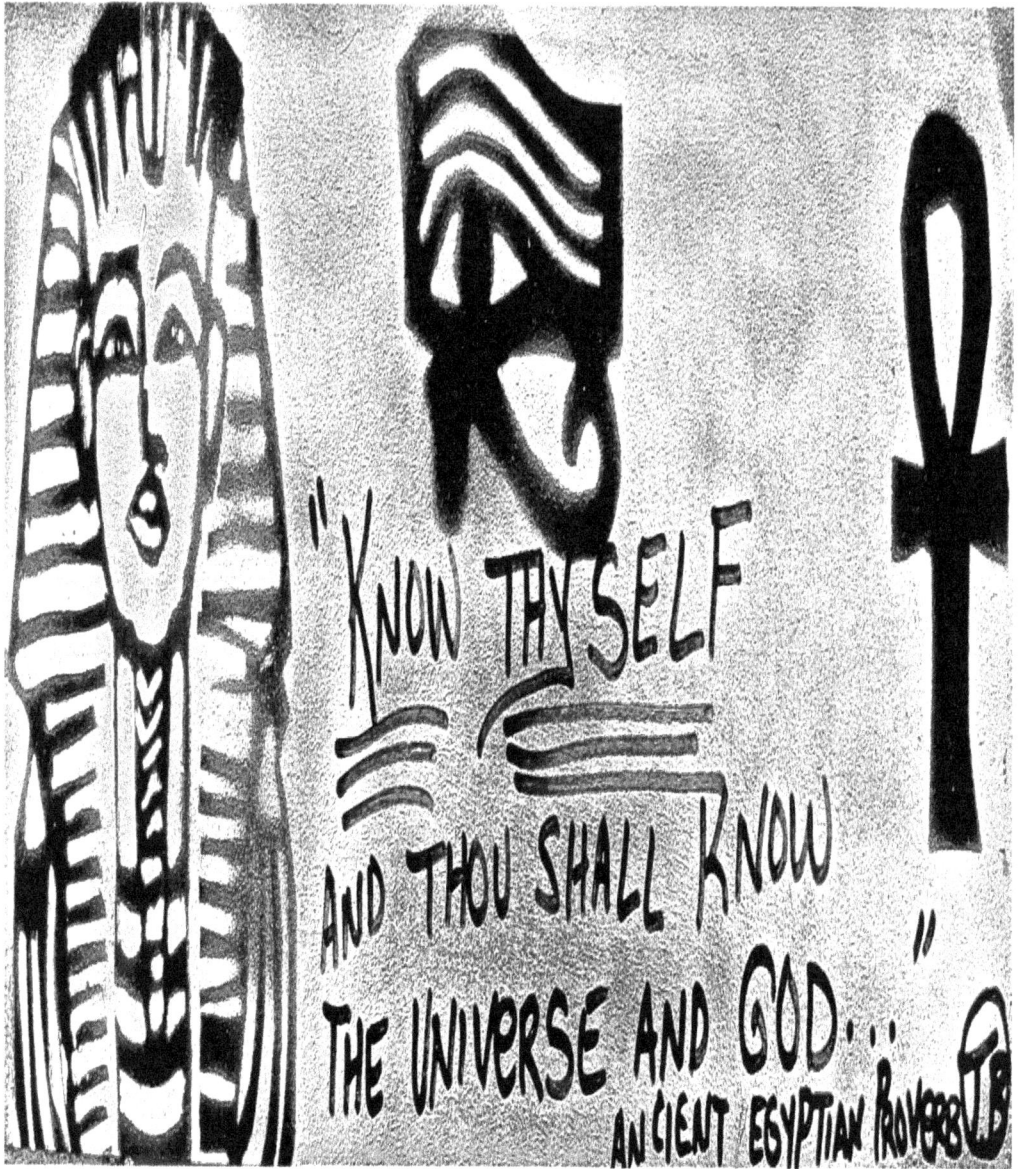

"KNOW THYSELF AND THOU SHALL KNOW THE UNIVERSE AND GOD..."

ANCIENT EGYPTIAN PROVERB

G.O.D

(Gift Of Divinity)

Whether Christian, Muslim, Buddhist or Hebrew
There's just one divine force that continues to rule
Call yourself a Baptist, Sufi, Yoruba priestess or even a Jew
But the CREATOR still recognizes the same G.O.D in you

See, we can all walk on the water and part the seven seas
Give sight to the blind and even cure all disease
Stop any famine, or do whatever we please
As long as we are truly connected and we sincerely believe

See, the breath of life is precious, yet, it's so often taken for
granted
As millions of organisms all co-exist on this one big planet
But there's one extraordinary thing we have
That other species cannot manage
And that's the power to create their own reality
Which we should use to our advantage

See, we've been blessed and passed the test, continuously
With a spiritual guide that lies inside of both you and me
And from the beginning of time, we've had great minds and the
G.O.D
The MOST HIGH energy, which gives us that GIFT OF
DIVINITY

NUMEROLOGY

There is but (1) Universal Consciousness
Flowing throughout everything
Divided into (2) energies Male and Female
Or the Yin and Yang

Within (3) planes of existence
In this (3)rd dimension
The Spiritual, Physical and Mental Brain
Moving in all (4) directions
North, South, East and West just the same

If we'd just use our (5) senses
We'd be able to Touch, Smell, Hear, Taste and
See
That (6) Protons, (6) Neurons, and (6)
Electrons
Produce the MELANIN in you and me

Powering our (7) chakras
Making (7)th Heaven a reality
The (8)th wonder of the world be you and me
And our Gift Of Divinity

With (9) holes in the body
And (9) planets in this galaxy
We are complete
Having (0) tolerance for negativity,
We be infinity
And the living manifestation of NUMEROLOGY...

JUST BE

So many people
Feel they've either gotta be this or gotta be that
A many people
See things as either right or wrong, white or black
A many people
Be caught up in categorizing and giving stuff names
When my people
You've got to just see everything is everything

So just be
One with Nature and Humanity
Just be
Cause we've got that Gift Of Divinity
Just be
One with the cosmos for eternity
Cause you are a spirit, so why can't you see
That all things around you are pure energy
So just be...

A many people
Be caught up in the trap of the material world
A many people
Lust for unimportant things like gold, diamonds and pearls
My people
All you have to do is sincerely know
All the abundance is yours and it will be so
If you believe in your soul, cause you're in control

We are Ancient
We are Peace and Love
Cause we are the Illuminated
And we have a connection with the stars above

So just be
One with Nature and Humanity
Just be
Cause we've got that Gift Of Divinity
Just be
One with the cosmos for eternity
Cause you are a spirit, so why can't you see
That all things around you are pure energy

DOG-N-GOD

The creator has always been, since way back when
Called a many things by a many people
But was named **GOD** by the European

Was it because backwards that spells **DOG**?
Which is supposed to be "Man's best friend"?
When the truth is that your only true friend
Is spirit that lies within

See, during the "ICE AGE" the **DOG** kept them warm
Like a blanket covering the snow
While melanated peoples were living in the pyramids
IN THE SUN, on the other side of the globe

We gave thanks and praises for animals
But wouldn't dare let them in the house
We saw them as a manifestation of **SPIRIT** and we loved
them
But wouldn't even think about kissing them in the
mouth

Nor would we put them on a leash and claim them as
property
We'd treat them as equals, yes indeed
Who also had the right to be free

But we never became emotionally attached
Though we were connected spiritually
We let them be and they let us be
As we coexisted continuously

However, the Caveman was forever grateful to the
canine

For saving him from the freezing cold
So the DOG became the Western man's DEITY
Back in the days of old

But WE ARE NOTHING AT ALL LIKE THEM
So we must learn to see through the fog
And ask ourselves "Are we truly praising the MOST
HIGH?"
"Or is our GOD a DOG?"

COMPUTER LOVE

I have a personal computer that I always keep with me
And there's nothing on the planet that I would do
Without my incredible P.C.

It's my best friend, my business partner and the one thing I
depend on
To get me through when I'm feeling sad and blue
And all my other friends are gone

It's my laptop, with an e-mail
That I take wherever I go
And when someone sends me a message
It immediately lets me know

I use it continuously, whether at home, work or on the road
Some say I have too much data in it
And one day it'll probably explode

I can't even stop using it when I eat or make love
So I've been told
People say "Don't you ever turn it off ?"
"Your computer's on overload !!!"
But programming it is the best part for me
Why ? Well, let me explain...
Not only is it filled with knowledge, facts and history
I also use it to entertain

Some try to convince me to shut it down at times
Exclaiming "You'll go insane !!!"
While others say it makes me too darn vain
Cause I occasionally use it to play games

But no matter what, I'll always love my computer

For with it, I can do **ANYTHING**
Cause the computer I'm talking about, can take **IBM** and
APPLE out
It's my **Divine Mind,** that you'll find, lies inside **MY
BRAIN...**

JUST A LIL' LOVE

When life has one down
With skies that are cloudy and grey
That's when
JUST A LIL' LOVE CAN GO A LONG, LONG WAY

A smile from someone passing
Might just bring some needed cheer
Or a few encouraging words in an ear
That someone needs to hear

An inspirational song on the radio
That brings back memories
Or a breath of fresh air
Accompanied by a gentle breeze

Anyone or anything positive
Might just brighten up someone's day
Cause yes it's true, for both me and you
A LIL' LOVE CAN GO A LONG, LONG WAY

So fill your days and nights with positivity
And share a fraction of your light with everyone you meet
Lend a helping hand, whenever you can
And give your spare change to a bag lady
Or a homeless man

Be a positive role model, speak to every single child
And sit and listen to the wisdom of your elders for a while
For, the more you give the more you receive
So let spirit guide all you do and say
And always remember that
JUST A LIL' LOVE GOES A LONG, LONG WAY...

THE GOLDEN TOUCH

Every since the days of antiquity
When the light of the universe first shined through us
We've been the Creator's greatest asset
And have been blessed with THE GOLDEN TOUCH

From the banks of the Nile river to the Mounds of Mexico
Our accomplishments are constantly being discussed
Though most of our achievements in history are shrouded in
mystery
Still forward we thrust

Following in the footsteps of our ancestors
Who were strong, proud and never ever blushed
Using the Divine Wisdom and our inherent ingenuity
We do for a many souls, just so, so much

And though some try to debate it and even hate it
While others try to keep it on the hush
We've never operated out of greed ego or lust
Which is why we continue to have THE GOLDEN TOUCH

From the construction of the pyramids without any tools
To the first royal garments, sewn with gold and adorned with
jewels
From Classical music, to Opera, Gospel, Jazz and the Blues
To R&B, Hip-Hop and Spoken Word Poetry expressing our
views...

Whether our hair be natural
Or we insert weaves, dyes, braids or give it a fade
Our elegance impacts and inspires the world
As we are forever on center stage

Innovating new styles daily
With not only our hair but the nails on our fingers and toes
Not to mention how we're mimicked due to our futuristic
fashions

Expressed through the art of us wearing clothes...

For, the spirit of KING MIDAS lies inside of us
And this is why we never fuss, cuss nor are in a rush
Cause just like a fine wine, we continue getting better with time
And know we'll always have THE GOLDEN TOUCH...

AMAZING GRACE

Every since the beginning of time
At the start of the "HUE-MAN" race
There has always been love, joy and peace
Plus the existence of "AMAZING GRACE"

From one seed came a tree, with roots and bearing fruit
Numerous and assorted, but with a delicious taste
Never, ever going to waste

And leaving permanent smiles on each and every face
Traveling the world over, bringing positive energy to every place
By the GRACE OF GOD, though some find it odd
Moving at a rapid pace

Leaving worries and fears behind, representing the divine
With the CREATOR as the foundation or base
And walking by faith, we never hesitate to state
That we are the living manifestations of that AMAZING GRACE

Gracefully evolving and problem solving
While our vibrations rise higher and higher
Our unity and strength grows and it truly shows
Especially when we see "GRACE UNDER FIRE"

Side by side, heart to heart and hand in hand
As a family, we continue to stand
Doing our best to build communities that are blessed
We give new meaning to the word "GRACELAND"

Made up of not only Kings and Queens
But as a whole we be the "Master Ace"
For they say "A family that prays together stays together"
And that's definitely true in our case

Cause the impressions and blessings we've left on this planet
Plus our traditions and offspring just can't be erased
We will forever illuminate every place and space
And exist as living proof of God's "AMAZING GRACE"...

THE MOTHER HERB

What is the one plant in the world
That when placed in the ground as a seed
Collects every nutrient one needs, but is still called a "dirty weed?"

One that's been here since the beginning of time
And all over the globe she grows
And she used to be the very fiber
That held together all forms of clothes ?

What plant has been used for EVERYTHING?
Even to heal most ills?
While the government claims she kills
Yet uses her to thread their dollar bills?

She can be placed in a tea bag and boiled
Or even pressed into an oil
And she never loses her potency, nor does she ever spoil

See this plant has been used to cure Asthma
Glaucoma and even Sickle Cell
She has liberated spirits, yet if you're caught with her
You'll end up right in jail

Some choose to smoke her or toke her
And they say she gives them a HELLUVA high
They claim she gives them a helluva high
So they can kiss this MATRIX goodbye

She was used in antiquity and a "Magic Root"
And is said to have a thousand and one uses
She's also considered to be dangerous by most skeptics
Yet, she's never taken a life through her abuses

But there's a many legends, myths and lies about her
However, despite what anyone's heard

147

For this metaphysical root, there can be no substitute
Cause she's the Original Nurse, MARIJUANA or HEMP

THE MOTHER HERB...

SPOKEN VERBS

Verbally and herbally filled with organics
Depth and weight to elevate or sink the Titanic
I never panic cause I'm a microphone mechanic
A New Age sage, serving the satanic

A St. Johns Wort and garlic, healing type of vibe
Is what I bring, no "bling, bling", nor St. Ides
My chakras spinning, from the beginning, with Mercury aligned
I'm the tingle in your spine, that's lighting up your mind

Kundalini, Kinetic, cosmic energy
The metaphysical secular, when you enter me
I'm andric, intergalactic, melanated and vegan
And righteous and rebellious be my rhyme and reason

Matriarchal, intellectual, well versed in heritage
Ancient as Atlantis, astrology's what I live
A carbon based creature, creative in habitat
Dark Matter Consciousness, preferring pitch black

Nucleus, brain cell, tissue salt, type of teacher
A fired free radical, forming full features
DNA decoder, head above shoulders
I'm outer space like NOVA, but colder and older

A subconsciously sinister, microphone minister
An astral plane dreamer, a Sirius B schemer
The Alpha and Omega, the Yang and the Yin
Gynamye, Akoben, with 8 layers of skin

Nine ether Bobashanti and a street Shaman
While clusters of confusion and chaos are kept common
Like Echinacea, Golden Seal, Peppermint and Eucalyptus
A bacteria breaker, I become when I rip this

Like Amaldahyde and Ammonia, I'm bringing the funk
A Kemetic continuation, condensed to an Ankh

And for all those who don't overstand what they've heard
You've just been sprinkled with a few of my Spoken Verbs...

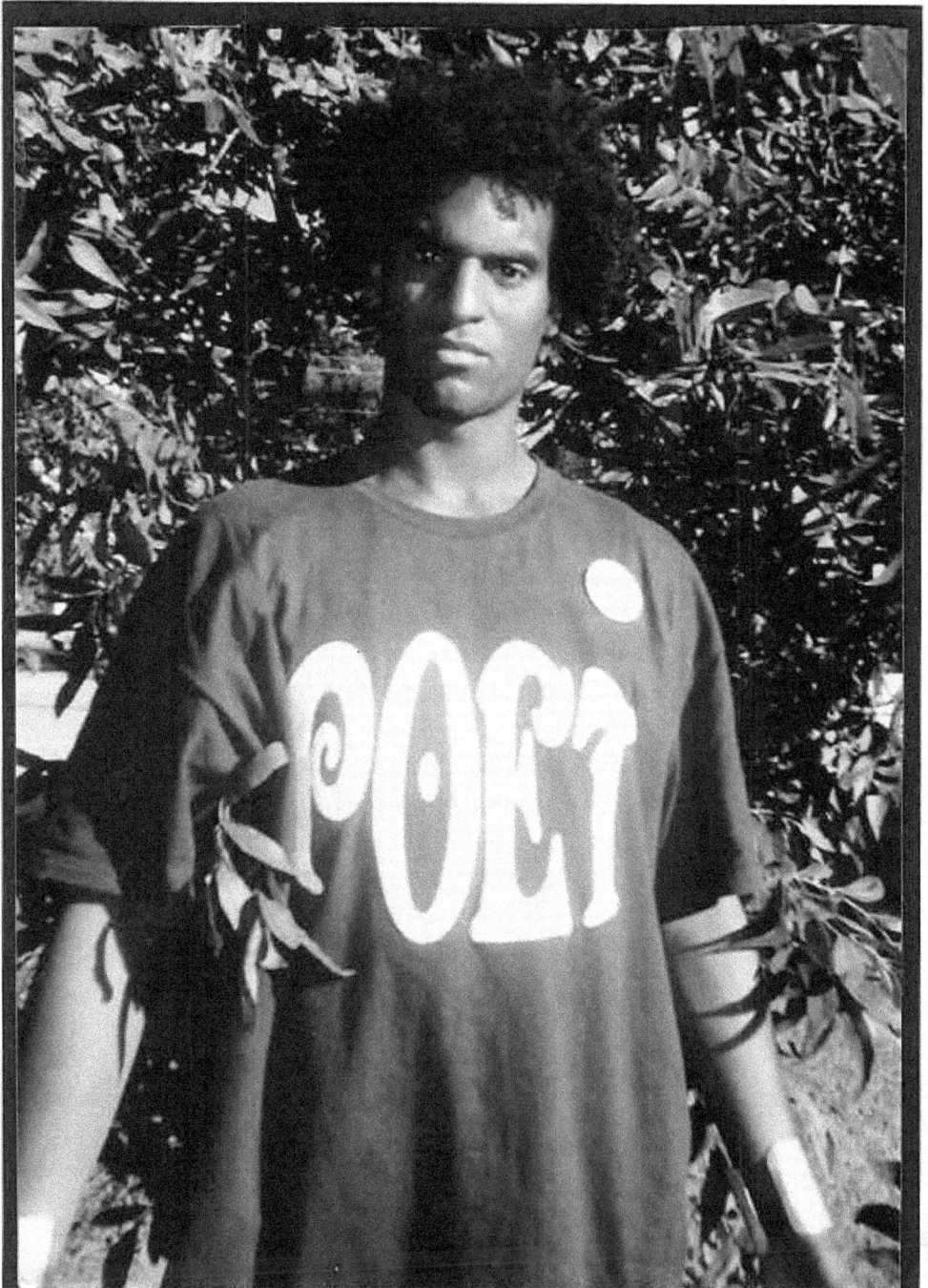

NO BUTTS ABOUT IT

As a strong Black man I've gots to do my duty
And say most sistahs be cuties, but my brothas are
into booty
What? I say a sistah could be educated, sophisticated
And have courage and guts
She could be afrocentric and authentic, but she's got
to have a butt
Now that's nuts...so for all my people not hooked on
phonics
Nor drunk on tonic, let me do some eloquent verbal
bionics...

See, since the birth of this nation, when we were on
the plantation
Black women have been subjected to all kinds of sexual
objectification
Every since she was spotted, and the cave man caught
it
And threw her on a ship
To the auction black, her value was not
Based on her mind but her behind, that's why she was
bought

She was called "sexually oriented", which was a term
the European invented
As an excuse to rape her shape, I'm sure, Cause he was
just that demented
Saying she was savage and impure, and sex partners she
would lure
Only so the cave bitch wouldn't feel insecure

So from the 1800's, Ms. Venus Hottentot, all the way
up to Hip-Hop
And from Prince and Michael Jackson to Mix-A-Lot
The African woman has always been demoralized and
degraded
And is so self hated, that she even reinforces the
stereotypes
Once she's made it

Claiming sexual Liberty comes with femininity

Like Lil' Kim, Foxy Brown and the rest of them
The system of white supremacy says she has no class
No morals, no values, no brain, just an ass

So, knowing this she utilizes it to the best of her
ability
Grinding with agility, having no humility
Saying her bigger, figure is definitely a work of art
While not overstanding why she's been reduced to being
loose
And just mere body parts

And this can be seen on videos, by rappers calling
them hoes
While 20 sistahs stand around in high heels and no
clothes
From "Rumpshaker" by Wrecks-N-Effects to H-Town's
"Knocking Tha Boots"
Not to mention Two Live Crew's Luke, It makes me just
wanna puke

Some say "I love our sistahs, I'm not into just
that..."
But these same brothas are always in the company
Of sistahs stacked not flat

But if you overstand, global white supremacy
You'll see that the Black woman's just being
What she's allowed in this society

Huh? When brothas call our sistahs gold diggers and
bitches
Is that what they truly believe they be?
Or are sistahs just acting like what they see
And are portrayed as on T.V.?

For, our Queens are being lied to visually
And the "tell a vision" shapes the perception of our
reality

So in actuality, a brotha like Mos Def who puts out
"Ms. Fat Booty" is still wrong
Cause if you want to uplift her, you never give a
negative picture
Or show her in a thong...you make her strong...

How? By letting her know ALL energy starts out female
And the original heaven is between the legs of a Black
woman
But this matrix is pure hell
And that she shouldn't believe in no Adam and Eve
Cause the Black woman never came from no man's rib
That's just Greco-Roman mythology

And the Black Woman's body should be covered up
For she was not placed here only as something to fuck
And her Pineal Gland is where a real man wants to tap
And she's destroying it and her melanin by
straightening her naps
Plus that she shouldn't throw herself at a brotha just
because he raps
For, her body is sacred, but her mind is infinite
And she should place more value on that

As for me, It's mental, that's the essential and I
can't live without it
For true Black Men dig sistahs with spirit within and
I'm one of them,
NO BUTTS ABOUT IT
And will I ever fall for someone because of her shape
Hmmm... I probably doubt it
My queen is an intergalactic melanated being,
metaphysically connected
NO BUTTS ABOUT IT!!!

FULL OF IT

It's 8am, you've just woke up and what's the first thing you do?
You get dressed, you shower and then you devour
In less than an hour, all the wrong foods...

See, most morning meals, do truly kill
Or upset your stomach and then definitely make you ill
So before you wake up and break your fast, with breakfast
There's just a few questions you really need to ask...

Like, "Am I truly doing and eating the right things?"
"Does cow's milk REALLY digest when mixed with grains?"
"Does boiled, I mean pasteurized juice have the nutrients I need?"
And "Why am I eating fruits that don't have any seeds?"

"Why are there 60 ingredients in this loaf I use for toast?"
And "Why is sugar in EVERYTHING? Is that what I eat the most?"
"Am I putting in my body, what my cells truly want?"
"Or am I eating out, just cause I like this restaurant?"

See, we are taught through the media and on our T.V.
In this society, to commit suicide nutritionally...
Cause animals don't ever desire fries, or otherwise, to go with
shake
And that's in just one area that we make a big mistake

What I'm saying is that a carnivore in the jungle would never, ever
state
I like this steak, but I think I need some vegetables on my plate
See, your digestive system needs riot gear to protect itself from all
the rocks
Not to mention all the chemicals you consume,
Sending your organs into a state of shock

You eat food sprayed with pesticides
Water full of chloride, sugar bleached and dyed
And then brush your teeth with fluoride, or rat poison in disguise
All as soon as you open your eyes, and usually all this is consumed
before 9:45

Then you consume yeast, which makes fat cells increase
Red dye #7, turning your organs burgundy before eleven
High Fructose Corn Syrup
Is that Natural or made in a lab somewhere in Europe?

And MSG, which is killing you and me
Plus causing brain deficiencies you can't even see...

And all this you've done to your temple
Before even contemplating eating lunch and dinner
Not to mention when your snacking, parasites be attacking
And you wonder why you're not getting any healthier or thinner
While people seem to be hungry as hell, with stomachs grumbling
and groaning
They walk into a store zoning, and pick up foods the FDA's been
cloning
And eat it late at night or early in the morning...

That's why it truly pays to eat organic these days
But who's to definitely say, even those foods are O.K.?

That's why you must never become a slave, to anything your body
craves
Buy yourself an enema bag or go and get a colonic, or do a juice fast
with a tonic
And overstand that ALL EATING IS TOXIC!!!

Plus try to watch everything that you come in contact with
For it maybe cloned or have hormones
Eat 75% raw foods and exclude, most cooked items not prepared in
your home

For, 90% of the population are FULL OF IT, I mean FULL OF SHIT
literally
However, for some it's just so hard to believe
That you actually are what you eat...

But you can eliminate waste without haste
If to your own self, you'd only be true
That's why it's always best to get with nature
Before nature gets with you

And don't get upset the next time someone uses that expression
Whether you be face to face, on the phone, near or far

If they say you're full of it, it's o.k. to admit
You just like so many others probably are !!!

THE SANDBOX

We're all like children playing in a sandbox
Learning how to spiritually walk and talk
While some just cry and others throw rocks
There are a few who just sit in a state of shock

Having come through the womb as a predestined portal
To this dimension we manifest as merely mortal
Searching to find the answers, our souls race against the clock
So we won't have to come back again to this spiritual sandbox

Watch as some build castles, while others literally eat the sand
And there are those who bury themselves in it
Plus those who try to command

All of the races and cultures are in it, from each and every land
Looking at each other strangely, while holding it in the palms of their hands
While some individuals lie in it and others choose to stand
We're all here to spiritually develop and learn to love our fellow man

For, our evolvement and transition depends on it
Otherwise to this realm we'll be locked
But as for this moment, though very few know it
We're all just children in a sandbox...

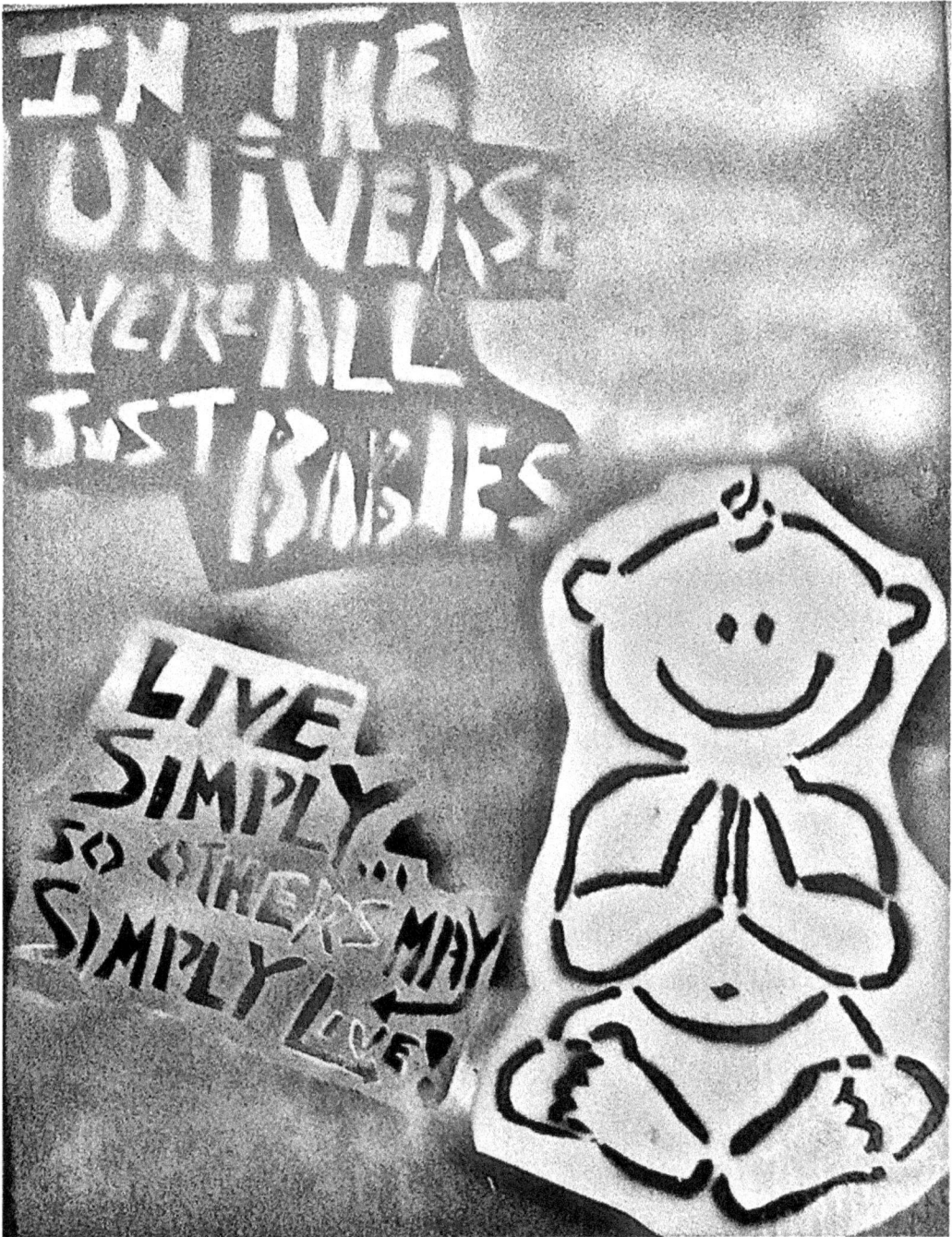

DEEP WITHIN

In the darkest hour of the night
Somewhere in the universe there is a light
Even in the coldest trenches of the bluest sea
There still exists a warm spirit that lives for eternity

As trials and tribulations seem to come and go
And disaster and despair fills the air high and low
It may seem like there's nothing that can change this
circumstance
But that's when you've just got to get out the way
And give the CREATOR a chance

There's strength so profound, that many never even tap
And an intelligence that's so supreme, yet it's sitting right
in our laps
As so many search the globe and truly haven't a clue
The very thing one seeks is already deep inside of me and
you

See, there's a force that allows us to maintain through thick
and thin
And we hear its voice directing us, time and time again
So there's no need to be down or walk around with a
lowered chin
Cause all of the abundance and power in the world is ours
And where's it at? It's DEEP WITHIN...

ONE

One mind, one body, one spirit, one love
One union, one heart, one CREATOR above
One chance one commitment, one sacrifice, one
vow
One place, one time, one future, one now

One kiss, one touch, one hug, one smile
One hand, one ring, one marriage, one trial
One bed, one pillow, one sheet, one cover
One friend, one companion, one partner, one
lover

One day, one night, one week, one month
One year, one decade, one moon, one sun
One thought, one mission, one philosophy, one
aim
One system, one language, one law, one game

One history, one legacy, one past, one heritage
One family, one nation, one people, one life to
live
One force, one universe, one planet, one star
One vessel, one energy and one destiny that's
ours

One search, one creation, one manifestation,
one call
One everything, one being, one existence, one
all
ONE ALL, ONE ALL, ONE ALL ONE ALL
All is ...ONE

CELLULAR MEMORIES

Transcend, don't stay, you spirit is ready
The problems of this world be too heavy

Mack truck, 10 ton, 50 elephant, concrete
Compressed into tears of a fatherless child
Running wild without a rites of passage
Juvenile system, flunky dropout artist, freestyling his way
through life
Swerving, ducking, dodging the feds
IRS, police with no license, but wanting to be legit, but for
who?

No parking validation, in this nation
Caucasians, Asians, Latinos, Blacks, Native American ancestry
Forced bloodlines, reservations, no rights to the land
Moorish sovereignty, killed at Columbine
David Koresh, World Trade Center bombed
Hip-Hops sister, sister twin towers, like Venus and Serena on
9-11
While working at 7-11

Tears I cry, for a communist country in a capitalist world
Looked at like the enemy, while oil tankers spill on the fish and
whales
And we starve in the Sudan and Somalia
While still praying to a white Jesus and importing Christmas
Trees and fat Santas

For children who have no concept of unity and love for self
Bleaching cream is second nature like vitamins
To Ghanaian and Nigerian women who invented the weave,
but not the lye and dye
That causes them to lie on their backs, while Barbie holds them
hostage
And sucks their breast milk dry...

But why do we allow such a barbaric system to exist?
Because we created it...

Colonizing leach infested Europe, a transient stench haven of
vomit and shit

While smallpox ran rampant, raw meat ate with poisoned fingers
While there legacy lingers...

To the New World, Third World be the First World
No retardation of heritage is complete
Without lynching, castration, decapitations and rapes
Calling the natives "monkeys, baboons, niggers redskins coons and apes"

As the tears of a tar baby drip like molasses off a fir tree
A weeping willow I be
While holding all of this pain and misery in my cellular memory...

MORTALS

Mortals make me mentally magnify
All of the absurdities in this dimension...

Mortals make me completely repulsed
At the thought of spending another millisecond
On this astroplane of existence...

Mortals are clogging up the portals of intergalactic
transfer...
Mortals are a cesspool of flesh all rotting
While their spirits stay frozen in a reptile like state...

See, only a mortal would believe that Eve came from Adams
rib
Having no knowledge or concept of Feminine energy
Nor the feminine principle of the universe
Screaming, "Oh lordy, trust in him and he will make
everything alright!!!"

Only a mortal would get stuck in some ignorant ass religion
Amen, Asalaam-Alakim, Shalom, Hotep type of
psychobabble book
Wanna be roadmap to the alleged kingdom
That seems to be anywhere and everywhere
But where they are standing right now...

Only a mortal could possible take a spirit in the flesh
And make them the sole communicator for the CREATOR
And worship the dead carcass even after the spirit is gone...
Jesus, Mohammed, Buddha, Krishna...

"The object is not trying to bend the spoon
But to realize that there is no spoon..."

Only a mortal sees supernatural powers as work of the
devil...
What is the devil anyway?   DAMN MORTALS...

Mortals see superhero, comic strip, space age action flicks
As the closest thing to actual supernatural powers...only in
the movies
Mortals build big monuments in the millions to GOD
But really don't have a connection to spirit

Hell... right after they pray, meditate or do whatever
They're right back in their old ways again

Mortals haven't recognized that spirit cannot be seen
It can only be felt...

Mortals believe, Mortals think, mortals assume
Mortals need visual proof, scientific evidence, and tangible
material
Solid facts, a book written by some scholar with several
letters
And titles attached to their name...

Mortals see spirit as OK, so...
How do I make money off of it?

Mortals don't see there is no separation of the All...
The ALL is everywhere, everything, in and out of existence
It is nothingness, silence, noise, chaos, peace, calm and.

Mortals are waiting to read a "How to evolve" book
Or see the paradigm shift on a HBO special, CBS Nightline

A Fox special report, or even on a rap video...

*Mortals are searching for the solutions to the world's
problems
In the Democrats, Republicans, the Vatican, The Wall
Street Journal
The New York Post and hell, even in the Vibe and Source
magazines*

*Mortals have gone and done everything in this dimension
But go inside, shut the fuck up and just be.
Be anything but...mortal
Ignorance is bliss
We are all mortal in one way or another
But we don't have to be, we have a choice to be like that
Or like this...*

SHINE BRIGHT

WHO TURNED OUT THE LIGHTS? WHO TURNED OUT THE
LIGHTS?
See, now there's complete darkness both day and night
So WHO TURNED OUT THE LIGHTS? REALLY, WHO TURNED OUT
THE LIGHTS?
What happened to the spirits that used to shine so bright?

See, we used to illuminate all things and were such a lovely sight
With spirits soaring and the heavens adoring us as we took flight
Until someone came and ran a game, punching a hole in our kites
And to earth we fell and were forced to dwell in our current plight

See, it's not our nature to have such behavior, for we know wrong from right
We used to spread love and an abundance of joy, not gossip steal and fight
But the candles in our souls have been put out and the flames have been
swiped
So now our essence we've forgotten and have turned to alcohol bottles and
crack pipes

But even despite our absence of light, we're gonna be alright
All we must do is overcome our fright and we'll reach new heights
And be able to reignite all our people's flames in this hour of midnight
So their spirits once again will glow within, and they'll experience that inner
delight

So WHO TURNED OUT THE LIGHTS? WHO TURNED OUT THE
LIGHTS?
Somebody used all their mite, to make sure we'd have a dark and dim life
But whoever turned out the lights, I said whom ever turned out the lights
Didn't know about our inner glow that was meant to forever SHINE
BRIGHT

FOREVER SHINE BRIGHT, FOREVER SHINE BRIGHT

So my people, I say there's so many flames that we must reignite
So that all the darkened hearts and spirits we encounter can also
FOREVER SHINE BRIGHT, FOREVER SHINE BRIGHT, FOREVER
SHINE BRIGHT

CAUSE WE ARE.THE LIGHT!!!

HALF EMPTY, HALF FULL

Life is either half empty or half full
It all depends on from which source of strength you decide to pull
Either it's headed for the light, or you're doomed in the dark
Because walking a tightrope isn't easy, but a work of art

Anything you believe in your subconscious, you shall come to see
You can be abundant if you choose, or broke as can be
You can live in health, vibrant and beautiful, without a single care
Or all you will attract to you is anger, pain, sorrow and fear

See, your choice must be made clear, before you even ask
"Is my life a half empty or half full glass?"
"Am I going to accept defeat or claim my victory?"
"Shall I live in a state of bliss or dwell in misery?"

And once your decision vibrates with your soul
And resonates in your spirit
Your aura will reflect it
And everyone around you will see it and hear it

Because you not being responsible for your situation
Is a bunch of bull
So just sit down and ask yourself honestly:
"Is my glass half empty or half full?"

HAPPINESS

When I look in the eyes of sistahs and brothas
Fathers and mothers of all creeds and colors
I don't see happiness, but sadness, yet still
We all wear a mask like our lives are being fulfilled

The material items we gain are supposed to numb the pain
But they only lead us back eventually to depression again
We try to use sex, sugar alcohol and tobacco plus more
As band aids to cover up our internal sores

But what's truly missing? That's the question we must ask
It's the lack of truly finding our GOD, which is a difficult task
One man's CREATOR, is another man's DEVIL
For, we are all here on this earth, but spiritually in different places
And on different levels...

The GOD within, for me, is not the GOD for you
That's why it's important to thy own self to be true
True and living divinity cannot be defined to a book
Nor a religion or set of laws, it's everywhere we look

Is our interpretation and worship of the most high?
Being influenced by this society and our oppressor's way of life?
Maybe that's why people I see, look unhappy and unfulfilled
Because their so-called faith and connection is forced and not real

Was the GOD of Columbus the GOD of the Indians?
Or the GOD of the Christian missionary the GOD of the spiritual
Africans?
Was the GOD of Hitler, the GOD of the Jews?
See, if you're thinking there's only ONE GOD, then for you I've got some
news...

The concept is great, but in reality it's odd
To think that in this 3rd dimension, there's only but one GOD
Societal pressures, organized religion and the very constitution
Makes one believe blindly and not seriously question morality and find
true solutions

So the dilemma lies in whether to have faith or self-doubt

Do we get to know our *GOD'S* within, or worship the *GODs* without?
Once we find our inner beings and communicate effectively
We'll all be better people and have a greater love for humanity

And there won't be as much sickness, poverty, death or even stress
While we'll all be genuinely fulfilled and possess internal happiness...

GOD IS IN THE GHETTO

Yo, Yo Yo Yo Yo...God is in the ghetto!!!
I said Yo, Yo, Yo, Yo, Yo, The gods are in the ghetto !!!

I stepped outside early this morning in the ghetto, walking down the block to the store
Thinking as I'm looking at the living conditions, GOD must not live here anymore
When sitting on the corner, with a blunt and a forty, dirty as hell with bloodshot eyes
Was the deity I'd been looking for, so I said "What up" and he said, "I'm the MOST HIGH"

So I said "Where have you been? I've been praying, meditating And looking for you everywhere"
"The preacher up the block claims the church is your crib" and he said
"Nah cat, I don't live up in there"
"That's where JESUS kicks it giving those seminars and running that big ol' game"
"On how to make a million dollars real quick, by franchising your name..."

"But you can check out my fam, they're everywhere, in every hood, any place you go..."
For we be with the poor righteous teachers, not the pork chop preachers
For the GODs stay in the ghetto

Yo, Yo Yo Yo Yo...God is in the ghetto !!!
I said Yo, Yo, Yo, Yo, Yo, The gods are in the ghetto !!!

So I went back to the lab, changed clothes and left my crib at about 10
Walked down to catch the bus on the corner, and saw that same ol cat THE MOST HIGH again
He was getting roughed up by some reptillians
Claiming he was loitering, panhandling and breaking the law
When out of nowhere came ALLAH, trying to sell me a bean-pie and a Final Call

*I had forgot I'd given all of my change to the MOST HIGH on the
corner,
And my dollars to JEHOVA this morning
See, JEHOVA be knocking on your door at 6 o' clock, the crack of
dawn
Trying to read you scriptures while you still sleepy and yawning*

*So I'm walking with ALLAH, asking about MUHAMMAD, who got
poisoned by the CIA in the ATL
When I see this cat shining shoes in front of the mall, who was it ? No
other than ISRAEL
He said HERU was teaching Egyptian Yoga classes,
And OSHUN was giving swimming lessons at the "Y"
YAH had a raw health food store in Atlanta and in New York,
KRISHNA got shot 41 times*

*BUDDAH was a D.J. in Detroit, But was still selling that good ol'
"BUDDAH BLESS"
While ATOM was a beatbox and PTAH an M.C., and yo his rhymes
were mad fresh
He could create shit just by his very words, and it would actually
appear
But the Masons were taxing fools for practicing spirituality
And had the whole hood full of fear*

*He said the ILLUMINATI were putting out tabloids about the
MECHELZEDEKS
And creating false rumors about the universal flow
But that's when I said "I'll talk to you later yo, I've gots more GODs
to see in the ghetto..."
Yo, Yo Yo Yo Yo...God is in the ghetto !!!
I said Yo, Yo, Yo, Yo, Yo, The gods are in the ghetto !!!*

*So next I headed over to this goddess by the name CALIFA 's spot
For, she be hooking up the tight ass briads and plats
While her homegirl MEDUSA did twists and locks
OGUN was in the building next door, hooking up the bomb jewlery
and metal cuffs
While JAH was sittin out front, listenin' to Bob Marley, rollin'up a
spliff
And then he asked me did I want a puff*

I was like "I'm cool" and that's when ISIS walked in,
Personifying beauty,100% natural but with so much sass
Talking about how she's raising the peoples consciousness
By giving a metapysical astrology class
Down at IMHOTEPs healing center, right after the African drum and
dance
Taught by ASHE' and YAHWE', with RA providing the lighting when
he gets the chance

But I told her I couldn't make it today, my schedule was full and by
the time it was done
I'd probably be at Club Kemet checking out KRIST
Performing his classic hits "South Bronx"
And "I'm Still #1"

But that's when LUCIFER rolled up in a fly ass Hummer on
20's,bumpin' "LIL JOHN"
Saying BEEZLEBUB was throwing a playalistic, orgy type jam in
Vegas
And if I wanted to go, I needed to come on...

And then who rolls up right after him ? some more REPTILLIANS on
bikes
Asking me for some I.D., and who I be
So I said "Me, I'm just a P.O.E.T, out her looking for my G.O.D.s"
And that's when they gestured and pointed across the street, right
towards the bank
They said "If you want to find GOD, he's in there all tied up,
And you can get him in DOLLARS, PESOS and FRANKS

And that's when I woke up from my dream
Completely drenched in sweat, thinking to myself, aw HELL NO
Cause I guess I forgot, whether we like it or not, Money 's also
another GOD in the ghetto...

Yo, Yo Yo Yo Yo...God is in the ghetto !!!
I said Yo, Yo, Yo, Yo, Yo, The gods are in the ghetto !!!

When you look at your people what do you see ?
An enemy or a deity ?
I know sometimes it's hard to believe
But everybody's a reflection of the G.O.D

REALITE'

What in my perception is reality?
Is it real or maybe just a formality?
Am I a victim, an observer or do I casually
Become a willing adversary or just a casualty?

Am I really in this skin? I mean is it truly a fact
Are they really white? And am I truly black?
And does a woman really make up, for what I lack?
Or am I whole, complete, right, absolute, exact and in tact?

My brain is processing 400 billion bits of information per
second
But I'm only recognizing 2,000, so I'm quite blind I reckon
If I don't continuously rethink all the thoughts I thought I
knew
And reprogram and rewire my brain cells through and
through

My paradigm only exists because I perceive it
And an event can only take place in my life, If I truly
believe it
Anything is possible if I truly can conceive it
And rewrite it into my cellular thought patterns, then I can
achieve it

But first I must override all the philosophical junk
That gives me identity and purpose and an egotistical funk
Cause even if I meditate all day or shroud myself like a
monk
I will still live the same life until my addictions are
debunked

What I'm saying is that these mere words are useless as can be
For they are but inhibitors and can't truly define
The inner workings of you and me
Nor can language describe that thing commonly referred to as G.O.D
IT JUST IS... But what else is? NOTHING... Not even this REALITY

ABOUT THE AUTHOR:

Tony B. Conscious

Hip-Hop / Funk / Rock / Soul / Spoken Word Artist

A renaissance man (Harlem Renaissance that is), **TONY B. CONSCIOUS** is the personification of AFRICAN-AMERICAN culture.

He is (amongst other things) A B-BOY, BEATBOX,EMCEE, GRAFFITI/VISUAL ARTIST (known as "THE GHETTO VAN-GO"), Poet/ Spoken Word Artist, Vocalist, AUTHOR, ACTIVIST, VEGAN VEGETARIAN and PHILOSOPHER.

AS a member of THE UNIVERSAL ZULU NATION, THE TEMPLE OF HIP HOP and AGAPE INTERNATIONAL SPIRITUAL CENTER, he seeks to use each and every element of HIP HOP to inspire, educate, motivate and redirect the inner-city youth and the HIP HOP COMMUNITIES WORLDWIDE to a place of balance, harmony, creativity, PEACE & LOVE.

He has not only worked for the OBAMA campaign (coined "The Obama Hip Hop Hype Man"), he has also been on stage and on tour with KRS-

ONE, GRANDMASTER FLASH, KOOL HERC, BUSY BEE, PUBLIC ENEMY, KOOL MO DEE, GRANDMASTER CAZ, PARIS, TUPAC and ERYKAH BADU just to name a few.

HE is and will be, until he passes on to the next dimension, truly the personification of **HIP HOP, Poetry, Funk & Soul music.**

DISCOGRAPHY:

DIARY OF A BLAKMAN. WORD C.D.	(1998)	SPOKEN
ESCAPE FROM L.A. WORD C.D.	(1999)	SPOKEN
UNPLUGGED WORD C.D.	(2002)	SPOKEN
(LIVE & UNCENSORED) WORD C.D.	(2003)	SPOKEN
P.O.E.T. WORD/HIP HOP	(2005)	SPOKEN
A PICTURE'S WORTH WORD C.D.	(2006)	SPOKEN
FREE THE JENA 6 SINGLE	(2007)	HIP HOP
KATRINA vs. WILLIE LYNCH SINGLE	(2007)	HIP HOP
I BARACK THE MIC RIGHT C.D	(2008)	HIP HOP/RAP
A.G.A.P.E HOP/SOUL/ GOSPEL	(2009)	HIP
ELV8TE HOP/HOUSE/FUNK	(2009)	HIP
HELP HAITI SINGLE	(2010)	HIP HOP
SAVE TROY DAVIS SINGLE	(2011)	HIP HOP
Lovely People SINGLE	(2012)	HIP HOP

BOOKS:

DIARY OF A BLACKMAN	(1998)	POETRY
BLACK HISTORY 101	(1999)	POETRY
100% NATURAL	(1999)	POETRY
BLACK LOVE	(1999)	POETRY
HUEMANITY	(1999)	POETRY
SPIRIT INSIDE	(2000)	POETRY
MASTERPIECES	(2002)	POETRY
A PICTURE'S WORTH...	(2006)	
POETRY/ART		
LIFE'S A BEACH (& then U die)	(2011)	
Autobiography		
How to Vend And Win !!!	(2011)	
Instructional Manual		
Do u Understand the words ?	(2011)	Quotes
* More Than Just Words...	(2011)	Acronyms
* (Always Resonating Truth)	(2011)	Art

(Still in the process of publishing)

MERCHANDISE:

CONSCIOUS ENTERPRISES	(1998)	Political
Apparel		
Fly Dye Art	(2002)	Visual
Art/Merchandise		
POETRY GEAR	(2005)	Spoken Word
Apparel/Accessories		

Barack Is Beautiful   *(2008)*   *Obama*
Merchandise

For bookings, products or other info:

CONSCIOUS ENTERPRISES/ FLY DYE ART

c/o ANTHONY BROWN (TONY B. CONSCIOUS)

1355 1/2 keniston Avenue La, ca 90019
Cell: (323)251-4969

EMAIL(S):   fly_dye@hotmail.com   art info
               Flydye_art@hotmail.com   Art shows

               B_conscious@hotmail.com Music, Poetry

               Teamobama@hotmail.com
      Obama/political
               Flydyeart@gmail.com
      International info

* ALL E-MAIL INQUIRIES WILL BE ANSWERED PROMPTLY.

ONLINE SITES & LINKS

Personal WEBSITES:

www.tonybconscious.com

www.flydye.com

www.flydyeart.com

www.poetrygear.com

www.beautifulbarack.com

Social Networks / Online Stores:

www.facebook.com/tonybconscious1

www.facebook.com/tonybconscious2

www.myspace.com/tonybconscious

www.myspace.com/flydye

www.youtube.com/tonybconscious

http://itunes.apple.com/us/artist/tony-b.-conscious/id290336359

http://fineartamerica.com/profiles/tony-bconscious.html

http://www.amazon.com/TONY-B.-CONSCIOUS/e/B006QWTTTO

www.sonicbids.com/tonybconscious

www.tunecore.com/music/tonybconscious

www.ourstage.com/fanclub/tonybconscious

www.reverbnation.com/tonybconscious

www.twitter.com/B_conscious

www.modelrun.com/actor/tonybconscious

http://venice311.org/venice-boardwalk/boardwalk-vendors-artists-performers/venice-beach-artist-performer-activist-directory/tony-b-conscious/

KEEP IN TOUCH !!!
TONY B. CONSCIOUS

www.ingramcontent.com/pod-product-compliance
Lightning Source LLC
LaVergne TN
LVHW061223060426
835509LV00012B/1400